JAIPUR

Author: Sanjeev Vidyarthi and Pratiksha Singh
Concept and Series Designer: Ariadna A. Garreta

First Published, 2018

ISBN (Bloomsbury India) 978-93-88134-57-6

10 9 8 7 6 5 4 3 2 1

Altrim Pubslishers
Passeig de Manuel Girona 55, baixos 2a
08034 Barcelona (Catalonia, Spain)
www.altrim.cat

in association with:

Bloomsbury Publishing India Pvt Limited
2nd Floor, Building No. 4, DDA Complex
Pocket C – 6 & 7, Vasant Kunj
New Delhi 110070 (India)
www.bloomsbury.com

Layout & Graphics editing: Núria Sordé Orpinell
Maps: Gopal Limbad
Editing and Proof reading: Neha Krishana Kumar
Photographer: Ariadna A. Garreta

Head of research assistance team: Ar. Yash Pratap Singh, Head of Department, School of Planning and Architecture, Poornima University. Drawings (digital recreations by the School of Planning and Architecture, Poornima University) and documentation: Ar. Chandrapal Singh Bhati and others (as cited on pp. 227-228).

Texts © Sanjeev Vidyarthi, Pratiksha Singh and others (as cited on p. 228)
Maps © Altrim Publishers
Photos © Ariadna A. Garreta and others (as cited on pp. 227-228)
Drawings © Altrim Publishers and others (as cited on pp. 227-228)

Cover Photo: Gatore ki Chhatriyan by Ariadna A. Garret

altrim
publishers

Indian
Architectural
Travel Guides

SANJEEV VIDYARTHI
PRATIKSHA SINGH

JAI
JAIPUR

B L O O M S B U R Y
NEW DELHI • LONDON • OXFORD • NEW YORK • SYDNEY

CONTENTS

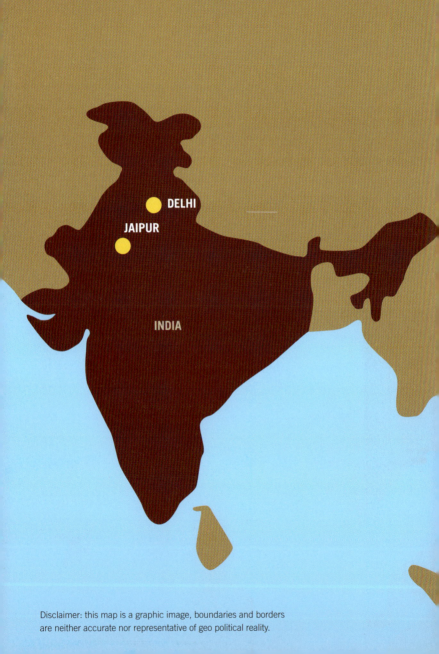

DELHI

JAIPUR

INDIA

Disclaimer: this map is a graphic image, boundaries and borders
are neither accurate nor representative of geo political reality.

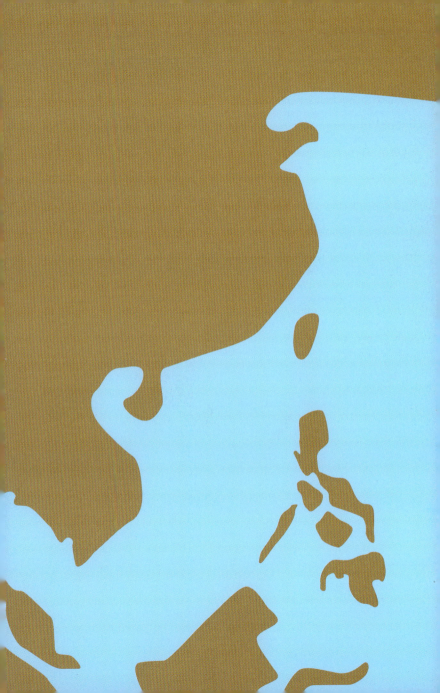

INTRODUCTION

The historic core of Jaipur is a unique place, unlike any other in the entire Indian sub-continent. The founders planned the original settlement both authoritatively and purposefully, conceiving a formal spatial layout demarcated by gridiron street pattern, and largely flexible internal spaces that could (and did) develop gradually per builders' changing aspirations and shifting social needs over time. The city's architecture also developed similarly, freely mixing a range of ideas and typologies from the regional building traditions as well as myriad influences that frequently shifted with changing princely whims, ongoing cultural exchanges, and external political considerations. However, the founding plan, conceived in 1727 AD, most influenced the city's architectural trajectory as it delineated the basic physical layout on the actual ground as well as established the template for future development. Below we briefly describe the backstory helpful in understanding some of the more important aspects of city's architectural development illustrated in this book.

We broadly organize the narrative along three major phases of city's development that the scholars of Jaipur have identified: Initial building phase that lasted from the founding to mid-nineteenth century, the approximately hundred years long period of British colonial influence from the mid nineteenth century to the mid twentieth century, and the more recent outward-focused developments following Jaipur's amalgamation with independent India in the early 1950s. Even as many driving forces overlap, and continuities and ruptures abound, the main utility of these three discursive phases lies in facilitating a quick overview of Jaipur's origin and long-term development while helping organize the following text in a lucid manner. Note that the origin and development of Amer, region's ancient capital succeeded by Jaipur, is not described here but illustrated in itinerary one.

Historic Jaipur was conceptualized before the idea of building new towns became commonplace in the rest of country during the subsequent British colonial and post-independence periods that witnessed many planned cities like New Delhi and Chandigarh. Incrementally built and thoughtfully nurtured under the caring gaze of hereditary Maharajas until their kingdom's merger with the republic of India, shortly after the country's independence in 1947, historic Jaipur developed through a distinctive approach to city-building. Architecturally well-known cities are usually famous for prominent buildings and popular public places. Chandigarh, for instance, is well known for modernist buildings designed by Le Corbusier within an overall masterplan approach while Barcelona is famous for La Rambla among other public places conceived by Juan Cermeño. Planned under princely autocratic rule, the walled city of Jaipur is most exemplary for long-term city-building via a pre-determined but internally-flexible spatial layout enabling the gradual development of architecturally distinct buildings and public places that ultimately cohere well with the urban whole. This feature stands out even more in contrast when compared with the typically disjointed urban form of most other Indian cities shaped by piecemeal growth and spontaneous developments over time.

Major design elements characterizing Jaipur's historical core are easily distinguishable and include: An overall physical plan that divides the city into nine squares housing different urban functions and diverse social groups; a formally conceived spatial order using gridiron pattern with hierarchal and wide roads; plan layout's Cartesian orientation (rotated about 15 degrees clockwise along North-South axis) in response to the local geography; strategically-located public-places like the two *Chaupads* (akin to a city square in the European context); landmark buildings like imposing *Havelis* (elite's mansions) and majestic *Mandirs* (Hindu temples) spread throughout the city; gradual development and widespread employment of a rich architectural vocabulary eclectically combining building typologies, spatial elements and elevational features sourced from a range of diverse traditions but painted

uniformly (hence the moniker 'pink city'); and a circumferential wall both securing the city, and regulating the entry of people, goods and commodities via impressive doorways (thus the use of term 'walled city' throughout this guide and local discourse, or *Char-diwari Kshetra* in Hindi).

Jaipur (combining two separate words: *Jai + Pur*) is named after the founder king: *Sawai* Jai Singh (*Jai* means victory and *Pur* means a settlement so *Jai-Pur* literally means the city of victory). Sawai (literally meaning worth one and a quarter [1 + ¼] times in strength and / or intelligence than a normal person) is an honorary title that Jai Singh, belonging to the Kachhawa clan of Rajputs who had ruled this region since the 12th century AD, earned from the Mughal court for unwavering loyalty and dedicated military service over past several generations. Founders of one of the largest empires in Indian history, Mughals were Muslim emigrants from central Asia. They cultivated close relationships with Rajputs, who were Hindus, for the reasons of social legitimacy and military strategy. Rajputs belong to traditional Kshatriya, or the military and ruling classes per the ancient tradition that organizes the society among four broad occupation-based and hierarchically-organized groups (or varnas) comprising Brahmins (scholars and priests), Kshatriyas (warriors and rulers), Vaishyas (traders and merchants) and at the lowest rung the majority Shudras (labor) who actually generated the extractable surplus working the hard jobs.

According to this social structure, Kshatriya kings were the customary custodians of *Dharma* (or value-based principles guiding this and afterlife) duty-bound to protect their subjects. Thus, tradition expected Rajput kings' close attention to general public welfare and, since land was the largest productive asset of the times, to overall planning and development of their territory. In this respect, the bonds between the king (especially if he was benign) and his lands and people were often intimate. Rulers were typically memorialized via the founding of new settlements (such as Jaipur) and building of public works (like the many lakes and step-wells located across this area). In the region of northwest India, where Jaipur is situated, rulers' land planning efforts invariably centered upon the judicious combination of carefully conceived water catchment and storage systems and the identification and development of defensible locations such as hilly terrain and hilltops (since this part of the world is climatically dry and frequently faced both external aggression and internal strife) and then setting aside suitable locations for relevant land uses like farming, pastures, forests, human settlements and sacred sites in line with the prevalent political situation, overall feudal system and the contemporary religious beliefs.

The combination of Sawai Jai Singh's enterprising nature and lucky inheritances along with the contemporary political dynamic played a key role in Jaipur's founding. On the one hand, once formidable Mughal Empire was just about beginning to disintegrate around the turn of the 17th century even as the British colonists, who would eventually replace it, were still sometime away from becoming India's paramount power. The transition opened a window of opportunity for regionally powerful players, like Jai Singh's dynasty of Kachhawa Rajputs, to claim new territories as well as consolidate their rule.

On the other hand, Jai Singh was a politically astute and practical minded king, who had not only learned from the diverse exposures serving away from home in the distant corners of the Mughal Empire but had also honed his repertoire of skills while augment-

ing Jaipur's already sizable royal treasury. He was also ambitious and willing to sponsor rather unconventional ventures like founding a purpose-built new capital city, experimenting with astrology, and conducting an *Ashwamedha yagna*—a holy ritual reserved for the highest ranking kings in the Vedic traditions. His ideas and actions shaped the walled city's origin and long-term development in foundational ways.

First, he employed his sizable resources to purposefully design Jaipur as a princely settlement both in its basic physical structure and architectural character. The act of building a grand city not only aimed at enhancing his reputation among princely peers but also to position his claim to eternal future fame by drawing upon customary religious practices. The spatial organization of the city plan itself draws upon key normative concepts described in Vastu Shastras (or ancient Sanskrit manuals describing guidelines for building towns and dwellings) that place the King at the metaphorical and geographical city center. Jaipur's massive self-contained palace complex comprising the royal living quarters and all the supporting services, attendant functions and key state offices, for instance, not only occupies the most important geographical location but also comprises the single largest parcel of land in the walled city.

Second, recognizing that city planning and building is always a long-term project, he adopted a flexible approach. For example, consulting many building experts per the legend, he chose the innately flexible grid-based spatial layout. Creating room for future possibilities, this act helped facilitate incremental building activity (often the royalty's favorite pastime), including the impressive temples sponsored by members of the royal household and the many palaces and pleasure-houses of various shapes and sizes patronized by succeeding kings and minor nobility, that could be (and were actually) built throughout the city as it urbanized. On similar lines, the grid also facilitated the quick development of Jaipur's famous bazaars along the major thoroughfares providing employment opportunities while the gradual development of inner blocks enabled the building of specialized neighborhoods housing occupational communities in close proximity.

As evident in Jaipur's plan, rest of the city surrounds and secures the centrally-located royal palace from all sides even as the planned layout facilitates quick access from the palace complex to other proximate land uses located toward the Eastern and Northern directions. These include the imposing hills forts of Jaigarh and Naha-rgarh conceived mainly for military purposes and the remarkable fort-palace of Amer that had served as the state capital until the founding of Jaipur city. As explained in Itinerary I, these forts are purposefully sited among a landscape of natural open spaces and rolling countryside dotted with forest areas, hunting preserves, formal gardens and water bodies of various kinds that collectively provided the playground for pursuing the outdoor pleasures of princely life. Illustrated in the second, third and the fourth Itineraries of this book, the architectural trajectory established by Sawai Jai Singh continued mostly unchanged until the advent of British colonial influences that arrived around the mid nineteenth century, described next.

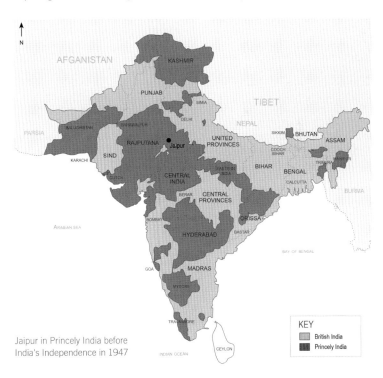

Jaipur in Princely India before India's Independence in 1947

Following British colonists' increasing pressure upon native kings to reform their feudal administrative systems and inward-oriented societies, Sawai Ram Singh (1852-1880) shifted the course of city's development trajectory by patronizing the building of 'modern' public works and promoting Jaipur's expansion outside the city walls. He ordered the creation of a public works department (PWD) appointing the prolific colonial engineer Swinton Jacob, who introduced the then prevalent 'Indo-Saracenic' architectural style into Jaipur's spatial form, while superintending many civic infrastructure projects that were evidently comparable to, and perhaps even better than those undertaken in

How much Colonel Jacob has done for Jaipur will never be known because the officer in question is one of the not small class [British colonial officials] that resolutely refuse to talk about their own work. The result of the good work is that the old and the new, that rampantly raw and the sullenly old, stand cheek-by-jowl in startling contrast. Thus, the branded bull trips over the rails of a steel tramway which brings out the city rubbish; that lacquered and painted Ruth [ceremonial cart], behind the two stag like trotting bullocks, catches its primitive wheels in the cast-iron gas-lamp post with the brass nozzle a-top, and all Rajputana, gaily-clad small-turbaned swaggering

British India's cities. These included road paving, municipal lighting, waste collection and water supply systems apart from the construction of schools, a museum, a public-park and a hospital. From a sleepy late-medieval settlement, Jaipur turned toward pursuing the orientalist image of a princely-modern city and in the process became increasingly known for its unique urbanity. Famous colonial writer Rudyard Kipling provides a vivid description of Jaipur's contemporary urbanity in his distinctive prose and determined style that deserves verbatim reproduction:

Rajputana, circulates along the magnificent pavements. (Rudyard Kipling, *Out of India,* 1895, 17)

Although Kipling's account certainly boosted Jaipur's romantic image, it omitted the key detail that the city's civic improvements were paid entirely by the royal treasury that also routinely paid all the municipal expenses. The city residents paid no direct taxes as well, and almost 2/3rd of state's revenue came from Lagaan, or different kind of levies and duties, extracted from the majority subsistence peasants farming arid lands in the countryside largely bereft of public amenities. Described in Itinerary V, this phase of city development, modeled after the colonial urban infrastructure improvement model, continued under the next two kings until Jaipur's amalgamation with independent India in the early 1950s.

As is well-documented, Independent India turned its back on the country's rich (but mostly feudal and bloody) history and looked toward a modern future under the leadership of prime-minister Jawaharlal Nehru. In the domains of city planning and architecture, this meant the building of more than 60 new master-planned

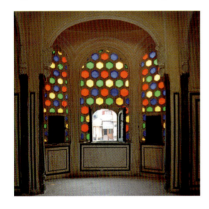

towns and cities like Chandigarh (see the Chandigarh guide by Altrim). Existing cities such as Jaipur, on the other hand, shifted focus away from their historic cores toward outward-oriented development adopting a comprehensive master-planning approach. The transition from the princely-authoritarian administration to democratic governance, however, proved strenuous as the newly-established Rajasthan state struggled with raising new sources of revenue while pursuing land reforms and abolishing feudal practices. Moreover, a

range of pressing concerns—such as the unification of former princely states, formation of basic administrative structures, and creation of new public institutions required by a modern welfare state —meant that the state government had little time and resources for other issues like those concerning the planning and development of cities.

Thus, not surprisingly, given the restricted attention on urban affairs, the government largely permitted, and even co-opted, many practices from the pre-independence period such as the state PWD's well-entrenched design approach and construction routines; while the left-out urban poor and rural migrants began building informal settlements as they searched for shelter and livelihoods in urban places. However, even as the PWD continued to build using the customary palette, Jaipur witnessed modernist developments like the Malviya National Institute of Technology (MNIT) campus described in itinerary seven.

A range of recent developments have begun to shape city's architectural trajectory in ways hitherto not encountered. These include the opening of Indian economy in the early 1990s; enhanced prosperity especially among the middle and higher social classes; growing flow of domestic and international tourists; proactive state support for public and private investment in growth sectors such as tourism and real-estate; and increasing social awareness about Jaipur's built patrimony. Apart from other implications, these larger socio-economic shifts have catalyzed conservation efforts for historical buildings and areas such as Hawa Mahal and Amer as well as the growing patronage for designing new places using the historic building palette. Itinerary VI, describing the development of 'heritage hotels,' illustrates some of the more notable efforts in this vein.

ABOUT THE GUIDE

This guide claims neither to be comprehensive in scope nor all-encompassing in nature. Like other architecturally rich cities, Jaipur houses a large spectrum of notable buildings and worth visiting places that couldn't possibly be included in a single book, with the probable exception of an encyclopedic effort. Moreover, we have intentionally not included buildings that are difficult to access by general public and visiting tourists. After all, what is the point in pointing out the most spectacular building, if you cannot visit it easily. Jaipur's many private residential bungalows, painstakingly designed by local boutique practices and regionally prominent architects for local elites and prosperous businessmen, are a case in point. However, we have made a conscious effort to cover prominent public places and important civic buildings, of course filtered through our own experiential knowledge about this remarkable and rapidly growing city, that the visiting tourists and inquisitive residents should find useful.

Unlike many other texts that focus mostly on the city's princely past, often reading it through rose-colored glasses, this book is premised on the simple notion that Jaipur is a living city. Rulers and decision-makers of the day, along with the many residents and users, built the city purposefully, incrementally, and continuously even as the many regime-changes, shifting social needs, and contemporary cultural preferences influenced their collective work. Thus, while not discounting the utilitarian importance of historical periods and architectural traditions, styles, and movements, we also pay attention to the larger social context that framed the development of buildings and places described in this book. Recognizing that architects often focus narrowly on the building as an object, we deliberately narrate local stories and offer historical insights that provide social meaning to these thoughtful acts of architectural design that ultimately contributed to city-building.

This book is organized in seven itineraries representing some of the most significant aspects of Jaipur's citywide architecture built almost over three centuries (1727-2017) including an entire itinerary devoted to Amer, the region's historic capital preceding Jaipur. Itineraries I to IV focus on specific geographies while Itineraries V through VII are conceived as transects illustrating specific themes and slices of the city. Collectively, they are designed to cater to a diverse range of architectural interests and to help organise your tour with respect to availability of time. Please note that some government buildings, like the secretariat and legislature assembly, require official permission. Best to plan your visit in advance through their reception centers / websites.

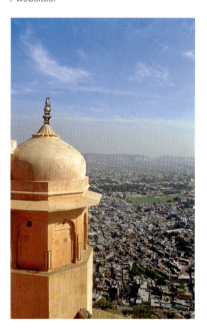

JAIPUR'S ESENTIALS

If you have only one day
to visit Jaipur:

Morning
Ajmeri Gate
Museum of Legacies
Tripolia Bazar
Hawa Mahal
Shri Ramchandraji Temple
Lunch at the City Palace Cafe

Afternoon
City Palace
Jantar Mantar
Jawahar Kala Kendra
Nahargarh Fort
Dinner at Nahargarh Fort

If you have more than one day:

DAY 1: AMER
Morning
Jal Mahal
Srijagat Shiromaniji Temple
Panna Meena ka Kund
Anokhi Museum
Lunch at Amer Palace
Afternoon
Amer Fort (Amber Palace)
Hathi Gaon (Elephant Village)
Jaigarh Fort
Dinner at Nahargarh Fort

DAY 2:
Morning
Ajmeri Gate
Museum of Legacies
Tripolia Bazar
Hawa Mahal
Shri Ramchandraji Temple
Lunch at the City Palace Cafe
Afternoon
City Palace
Jantar Mantar
Shri Ramchandraji Temple
Gaitor Ki Chhatriyan
Jawahar Kala Kendra

If you have more time:

DAY 3
Morning
Jal Mahal
Ghat ki Guni
Sisodiya Rani Ka Bagh
Vidhyadhar Ka Bagh
Lunch at Lebua Resort
Afternoon
Albert Hall Museum
Raj Mandir Cinema
Panch Batti and MI Road
Dinner at MI Road (Niros, Natraj, Surya
Mahal or Grand Chanakya)

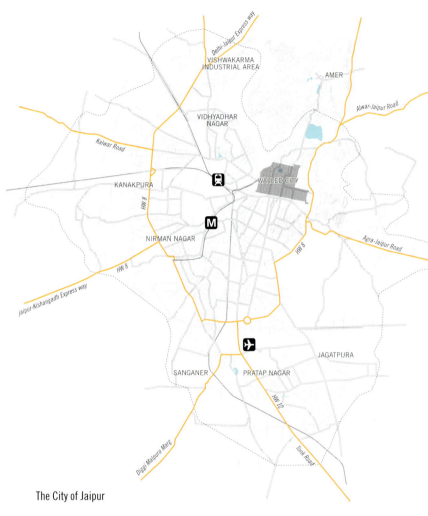

The City of Jaipur

Capital of Rajasthan State
Area: 467 km^2. (180 sq mi)*
Population (2011)*: 3,046,189**
Density: 6,500/km^2 (17,000/sq mi)**
Census of India. Retrieved 10 February 2016.
*Jaipur Municipal Corporation. Retrieved 24 April 2018.

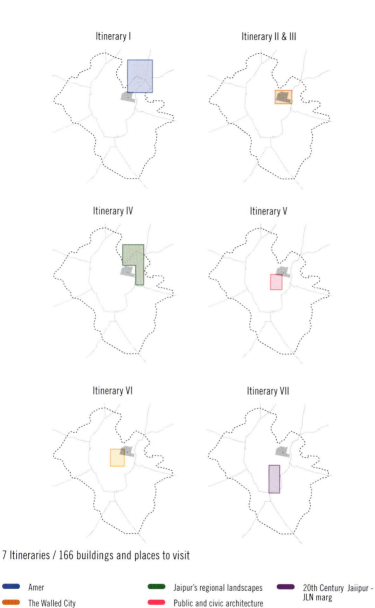

Itinerary I

Itinerary II & III

Itinerary IV

Itinerary V

Itinerary VI

Itinerary VII

7 Itineraries / 166 buildings and places to visit

- Amer
- The Walled City
- Havelis, markets, arts and crafts
- Jaipur's regional landscapes
- Public and civic architecture
- Heritage Hotels
- 20th Century Jaiipur - JLN marg

Starting Point

Jorawar Singh Gate

1. Amer Fort and Palace Complex
   - 1.1 Jaleb Chowk
   - 1.2 Diwan-i-aam
   - 1.3 Aaram bagh
   - 1.4 Jai Mandir
   - 1.5 Zenana
2. Panch Mukhi Mahadev Mandir
3. Chomu Haveli
4. Sri Jagat Shiromaniji Temple
5. Ambikeshwar Mahadev Mandir
6. Chood Singh Haveli
7. Panna Meena ka Kund
8. Bihari ji ka Mandir
9. Anokhi Museum
10. Sagar Lake
11. Akbari Mosque
12. Bharmal ki Chhatri
    (Kachhawa Cenotaphs)
13. Hathi Gaon (Elephant Village)

Additional buildings:

A. Pearl institute

B. Lebua Lodge Amber

Cafes and Restaurants:

Anokhi Museum

Anokhi Haveli, Kheri Gate

Cafe Coffee Day

Amer Fort Restaurant 1135 AD, Amer Fort

Restaurant 1135 AD, Amer Fort

Toran Restaurant, Lebua Lodge Amber, Jaipur
Kunda, NH-8 Tehsil, Amer

www.lebua.com

Shopping:

CMYK Bookstore, gifts and souvenirs shop,
Amer Fort

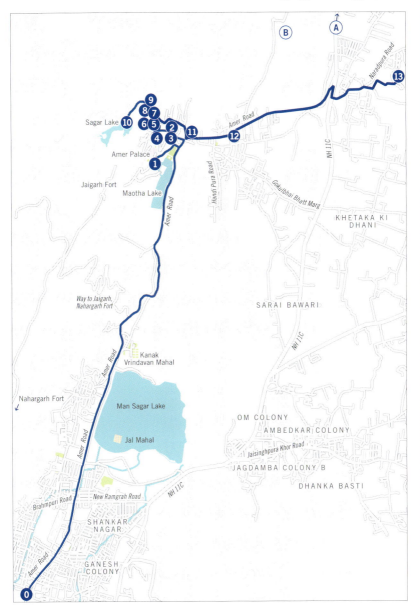

Sagar Lake

Amer Palace

Jaigarh Fort

Maotha Lake

Amer Road

Way to Jaigarh,
Nahargarh Fort

Kanak
Vrindavan Mahal

Amer Road

Nahargarh Fort

Man Sagar Lake

Jal Mahal

OM COLONY

AMBEDKAR COLONY

Jaisinghpura Khor Road

JAGDAMBA COLONY B

DHANKA BASTI

SARAI BAWARI

KHETAKA KI
DHANI

Gokulbhai Bhatt Marg

Handi Pura Road

Amer Road

Naradpura Road

NH 11C

New Ramgrah Road

NH 11C

Brahmpuri Road

SHANKAR
NAGAR

GANESH
COLONY

Amer Road

0m   20m   1km   N

zoom

⑨

⑧⑦

⑥⑤

Sagar Lake ⑩

②

④ ③

⑪ Amer Road

⑫

Amer Palace

①

Jaigarh Fort

Maotha Lake

Rain Water Reservoir

Amer Road

Handi Pura Road

Way to Jaigarh,
Nahargarh Fort

Nahargarh Fort

Amer Road

Kanak
Vrindavan Mahal

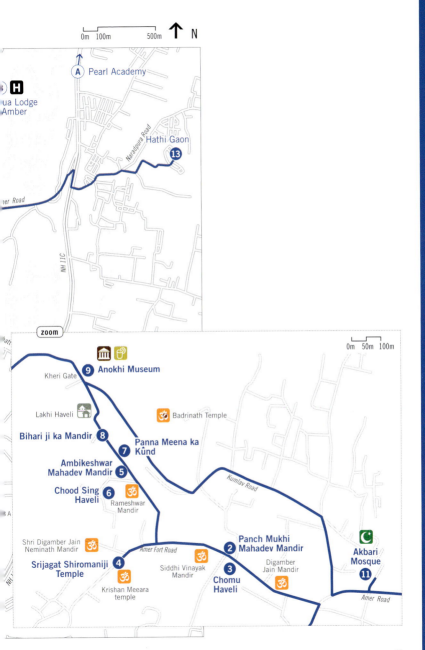

0m 100m 500m

N

(A) Pearl Academy

H
ua Lodge
Amber

Narainpura Road

Hathi Gaon

13

ner Road

NH 11C

zoom

0m 50m 100m

🏛 🍹

9 Anokhi Museum

Kheri Gate

Lakhi Haveli 🏠

🕉 Badrinath Temple

Bihari ji ka Mandir 8

7 Panna Meena ka Kûnd

Ambikeshwar Mahadev Mandir 5

Kumlav Road

Chood Sing Haveli 6
🕉 Rameshwar Mandir

Shri Digamber Jain Neminath Mandir 🕉

Panch Mukhi Mahadev Mandir 2

🇵🇰
Akbari Mosque

Srijagat Shiromaniji Temple 4
🕉
Amer Fort Road
🕉 Siddhi Vinayak Mandir

Digamber Jain Mandir

11

Krishan Meeara temple

3 Chomu Haveli

🕉

Amer Road

Starting Point **Jorawar Singh Gate** 15th C.

Jorawar Singh Gate, Chokdi Gangapol

ITINERARY LEVEL: Medium (by car/foot)
DURATION: one day
DISTANCE: around 4-5 km

PRACTICAL INFORMATION:

The Palace Complex and major monuments are open to the public. There is an entry fee. See 'Monuments Timings' p. 210, for details.

Most of the temples are open to the public from early morning till evening. Unfortunately most of the havelis and private propieties are not open to the public but no harm asking.

Anokhi Museum
www.anokhi.com/museum/

DRONAH Foundation
Foundation 'Amber Heritage Walk':
www.dronahfoundation.org/heritage-walk/

Amer is the historical capital of this region. The forts and supporting settlement of Amer go back many centuries prior to the founding of Jaipur city in 1727 AD. *Kachhawa* Rajputs defeated Meena chieftains, who were the original founders of Amer, in the early years of the second millennium after Christ, establishing the ruling dynasty that lasted a long time—until the abolition of princely rule accompanying India's independence in 1947. Amer, however, grew in importance, size, and population after the *Kachhawa* Kings became close to the Mughal rulers from the XVI century onwards, eventually becoming so influential and prosperous that they could afford (both politically and financially) to shift their capital to the brand-new city of Jaipur developed in proximity to the principal Mughal city of Delhi. Therefore, in sharp contrast with the comprehensively conceived city plan and refined architecture of Jaipur, Amer not

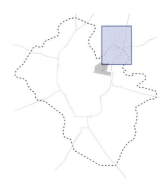

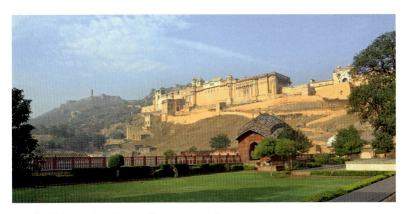

Amer Fort-Palace on the hill, behind it stands Jaigarh Fort.

only exhibits incremental development over time but also the militaristic orientation of medieval India. So, while following this itinerary, observe the hilly landscape that surrounds Amer area. Paying attention to Amer's overall setting is important because the builders have worked closely with the terrain and geographical features, like the natural depressions, valleys and inclines, for a variety of reasons such as the area's military defense and water catchment and storage, while carefully siting the human settlements and forts among forests and open areas because hunting was a favorite royal pastime. Notice how the nature and water play important roles through out this territory as you encounter them in various locations and forms, mostly showcased in itinerary V. The itinerary also includes more recent buildings illustrating renewed interest in the Amer area that witnessed little development activity until recently.

1. Amer Fort and Palace Complex - 967 CE - 15th C.

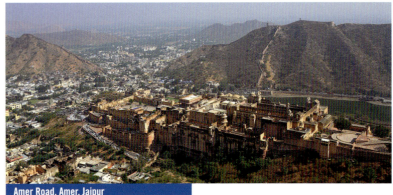

Amer Road, Amer, Jaipur

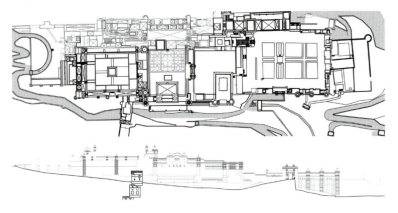

Site plan and elevation

For many visiting tourists, Amer is Jaipur's main attraction. Located about 10 kilometers from the city center, Amer is the region's ancient capital that gained prominence and stature during the 16th century under Raja Man Singh, who nurtured strategic ties between the Rajputs and the powerful Mughal empire needing regional alliances to expand further. Serving the Mughals, both as an army general and provincial governor in many different parts of the country, Man Singh gained substantial cultural exposure and material wealth that he diligently employed to develop his hometown of Amer. Supported by an older settlement built along a narrow valley toward the north and northwestern side, the dramatically sited hillfort of Amer exemplifies his life-experience and worldview in two important ways. First, the Amer fort-palace, combining the functions of a military fort and royal place, is built to im-

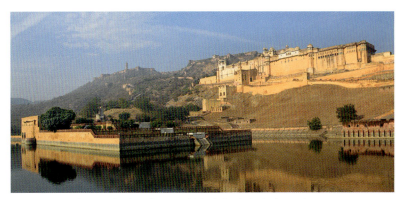

Kesar Kyari Bagh, Maota Lake, Amer Palace and Jaigarh Fort in the background

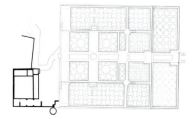

Kesar Kyari Bagh garden plan

press, and continues to do so even today. The spectacular massing and visual composition of the spatial form leveraging the hilltop location, the purposeful fit with the surrounding landscape, the inclined approach uphill via a series of imposing gateways, the sheer human effort employing basic building tools and rudimentary construction techniques over many decades, and the massive physical scale of the development, completely outsizing the original settlement of Amer, all bear testimony to the builders' fantastic ambitions. Second, Amer fort-palace combines design elements and planning features from the Rajput and Mughal traditions creating an inventive royal campus offering an impressive range of multiple living, working, and recreational opportunities (especially when compared to the actual needs of the tiny royal population that it was designed to serve) perhaps unmatched in other hillforts of India.

1.1 Jaleb Chowk Maharaja Sawai Jai Singh - 1699-1743

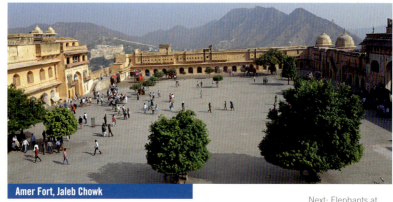

Amer Fort, Jaleb Chowk

Next: Elephants at Jaleb Chowk and ride on the cobbled pathway to the fort; Diwan-i-Aam, and the magnificent Ganesh Pol detail and full view (Clockwise from top left).

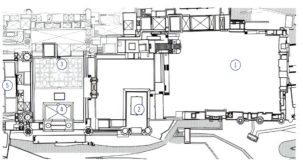

1. Jaleb Chowk
2. Diwan-i-aam
3. Aaram bagh
4. Jai Mandir
5. Zenana

Plan

Serving both the main entrances into the fort, *Jaleb chowk* is the largest single space in the entire palace. Conceived as an open-to-sky courtyard surrounded by perimeter buildings, this space housed diverse facilities and offices requiring public interaction. The space is clearly designed to impress both the noble guests as well as the commoners visiting for official business or awaiting attendance at the princely court. The word Jaleb is ostensibly of Persian origin and carries a military connotation. Given the spatial layout, it is clear that the builders envisaged this space for cavalry drills and royal salutes in addition to the occasional large gatherings during a religious event or royal celebration. Jaleb chowk also facilitates access to other areas that a commoner might visit such as the Diwan-i-aam (described next) and the Shila Mata temple. Most commoners would simply not be allowed beyond these locations customarily guarded by armed sentries.

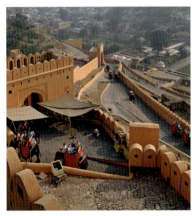

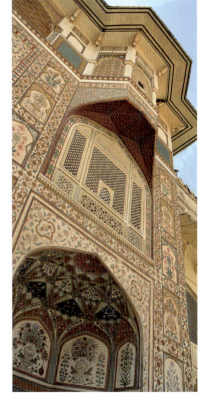

1.2 **Diwan-i-aam** Maharaja Sawai Man Singh - 1589-1614

Amer Fort, Amer Road

Diwan-i-aam translates as the hall for public audience. A signature typology of Mughal architecture, similar examples of which exist in Delhi and Agra, it is built with regionally available sandstone used in intri-cately carved arches and a total of forty columns. Many surfaces were plastered with a mix of fine lime and sea shell powders that were rubbed intensely upon drying to obtain marble like finish.

1.3 **Aaram bagh** Maharaja Sawai Jai Singh - 1699-1743

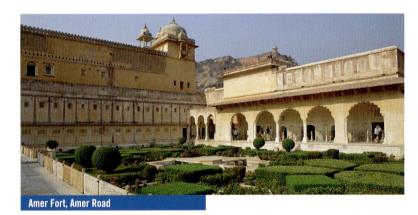

Amer Fort, Amer Road

Again, borrowed from the Mughal landscape traditions (also called the Char Bagh pattern), Aaram bagh means the garden meant to rest. Abutting the Jai Mandir, it offered one of the several options for royal recreation. It has been recently restored along with other conservation works by the Ahmedabad-based architect Meenakshi Jain.

1.4 Jai Mandir Maharaja Sawai Jai Singh - 1621-1667

Amer Fort, Amer Road

Jai Mandir means the hall of victory, and along with the adjoining *Sukh Niwas* (literally the house of pleasure), it formed Maharaja's personal quarters. You enter the decorated hall with carved marble panels and multi-mirrored ceiling via Ganesh pole decorated with frescoed arches. From Jai Mandir, you can enjoy sweeping views of the Maota lake below and the surrounding landscape.

1.5 Zenana Maharaja Sawai Man Singh - 1580

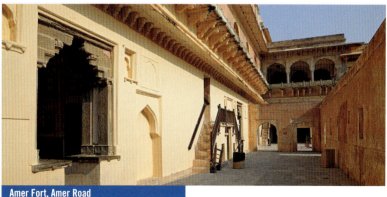

Amer Fort, Amer Road

Zenana means ladies' quarters and this space was reserved exclusively for the royal women and their female companions. Social protocol dictated strict segregation of sexes and no male, other than the Maharaja, could enter these premises guarded around the clock by armed, and typically third-gender, guards.

2. Panch Mukhi Mahadev Mandir

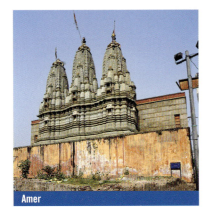

Amer

Many members of Jaipur's ruling family were avowedly religious and thus sponsored many temples throughout Amer and Jaipur for a variety of reasons. Thus, you'll frequently encounter a diverse range of architecturally distinct temples dedicated to different deities of the Hindu pantheon. Paanch Mukhi Mahadev is one such shrine dedicated to Shiva featuring a distinctive five-faced Shivling or Shiva's symbol.

3. Chomu Haveli Govind Singh - 1901

Amer

Politically and administratively, Jaipur, similar to other Rajput kingdoms, was organized in areas ruled directly by the state (called *Khalsa*) and *Thikanas*, or largely autonomous rural regions typically ruled by members of the ruling dynasty. One of the highest ranking noble families, ruled Chomu, located about 30 kilometers from Jaipur.

4. Sri Jagat Siromaniji Temple Rani Kankawati - 1599-1608

Amer

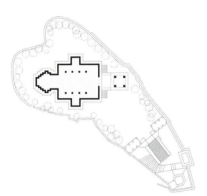

Site plan

Jagat Siromani, meaning the 'lord of the world,' is one of the more beautiful temples of Amer built with local materials. Per popular legend, it was sponsored by one of the queens of Maharaja Man Singh I in the memory of their son Jagat Singh. She must have loved him dearly for this is a magnificent temple with a very impressive entrance. The particularly tall and imposing entrance gate, resembling a *gopuram*, is rather uncommon for North India and is usually found in the temples of country's southern peninsula. Moreover, this temple is strategically located on an elevated site and the juxtaposition of two elephant statues creates an inviting and welcoming entrance from the street level. Dedicated to Vishnu, and one of Vishnu's famous reincarnations is the popular *Bhagwan Krishna*, the temple also celebrates the memory of one of his most devout and well-known female followers called Meera.

5. Ambikeshwar Mahadev Mandir Maharaja Ranjit Singh - 1822-1860

Amer

One of the oldest temples in Amer. Some legends call it thousands of years old while others link it to the origin of Amer itself, as evident in the resemblance between the words 'Amer' and 'Ambikeshwar' (literally the 'lord of Amer'). However, the curious mix of facts that: it is neither ornate nor impressive, definitely old, and sunken below the street level, but still in use while missing a well-documented history do add up to a certain mystery. You enter the temple through the Ambikeshwar chowk, or a large public plaza, denoting a historic recognition associated with the place. The principal deity is Shiva, but several other idols installed as well. Visit if you are a history buff and appreciate the architectural notion of 'palimpsest,' or the idea that later additions built on top of previous building layers often try to efface the earlier ones even as historical traces remain.

6. Chood Singh Haveli

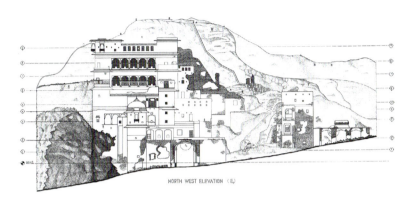

NORTH WEST ELEVATION (E₁)

Elevation

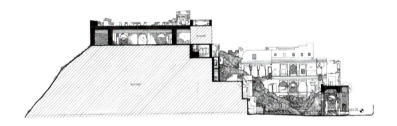

Section

Chood Singh Haveli means the mansion of Chood Singh. Located in strategic proximity to the Amer Fort and its access road, this place comprises majestic ruins of a historical property belonging to a nobleman who most probably held an important position either in the princely hierarchy or the royal court. Designed as a 'U' shaped building centered upon an open-to-sky courtyard, part of the structure rises to an impressive seven stories creating an imposing effect. Visiting this place not only gives you a firsthand feel of the gradually unfolding abandonment and dereliction Amer faced in the wake of Jaipur's emergence as the most important city in this region but also the general neglect of heritage buildings in contemporary India. Many historically significant private properties, like the *Chood Singh Haveli,* lack owners or clear title documents and are often occupied by renters or encroachers, who frequently contest conservation and redevelopment efforts.

7. **Panna Meena ka Kund** Panna Meena - 1699-1743

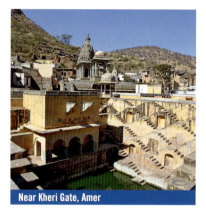

Near Kheri Gate, Amer

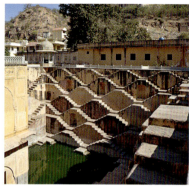

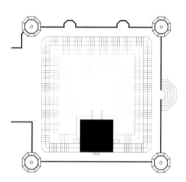

Plan

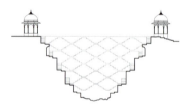

Section

Panna Meena ka Kund is a step well. Step wells are manmade water storage structures using an inverted form of architecture built deep into the terrain rather than above the ground. They are also a prototypical feature of water planning in climatically dry region of Northwestern India that includes the Rajasthan state and adjoining areas. Water is critical for survival in this arid expanse that frequently encounters little rains and long droughts. So, the fundamental function of step wells is to store rainwater for nearby populations and passersby. But, due to their clever architecture comprising all-around steps, covered pavilions, wide platforms and cool resting areas, they also served as public and community spaces offering opportunities to interact, rest, and seek refuge from the scorching sun. Thus, rich patrons and local elites, such as Panna Meena, often sponsored stepwells for the purpose of public charity and memorializing the family name.

8. Bihariji ka Temple

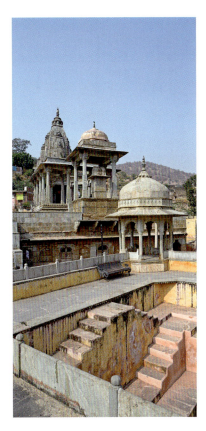

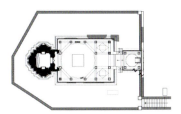

Plan

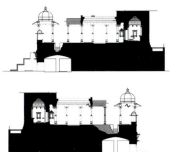

Sections

Bihari Ji Ka Mandir is a partly dilapidated temple offering an excellent example of 17th century temple architecture (or the so-called *Nagara style*) in this region. However paradoxically, the purpose of including this semi-derelict temple in the itinerary is that here you can observe the local construction techniques used for temple building. The three structural parts of the temple are clearly evident: the entrance or *ardhmandapa* which is intact, the *mandapa* or the congregation hall with supporting stone pillars and the missing roof; and the impressive *shikhara*, the tallest part of the temple below which lies the *garbhagriha*, or the inner sanctorum that houses the deity. It is also important to note that, after decades of neglect, public authorities and non-profit agencies are now beginning to pay attention to the temple's upkeep and conservation in line with the broader societal trend of growing concern and appreciation for this country's built heritage.

9. Anokhi Museum Ar. Parul Zaveri and Nimish Patel (restoration) - 1970-1989

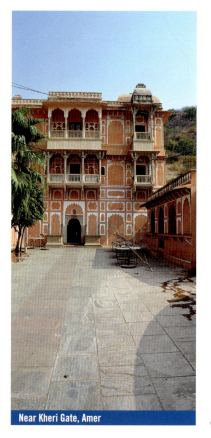

Near Kheri Gate, Amer

Sections

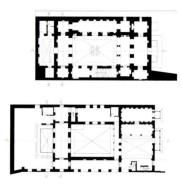

Ground and second floor plans

Anokhi Museum showcases the craft of hand block printed fabric in a carefully-restored historical haveli. Haveli was the prototypical dwelling of higher social classes in this part of the world before the colonial bungalow replaced it under British influence. Culturally-sensitive Jaipur-based entrepreneurial couple called Faith and Jitendra Pal (John) Singh, founded a boutique clothing company named Anokhi in the 1970s that sought to promote the diminish-

ing practice of hand block printing. Jaipur and surrounding places like Sanganer and Bagru are famous for this craft using organic colors and hand-made wooden blocks. Engaging Ahmedabad based architects, committed to conserve and promote local building traditions, Parul Zaveri and Nimish Patel, Anokhi bought and painstakingly restored this largely dilapidated structure in the early 1990s.

10. Sagar Lake Maharaja Sawai Man Singh - 1610

Sagar Road, Amer

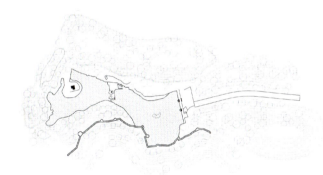

Site plan

Sagar literally means sea. Sagar's significance lies in the thesis that: City-builders first planned for water and then sited and developed human settlements and associated land uses in this arid region. Proximate water bodies like the Man Sagar lake, Maota, Panna Meena ka Kund and the Sagar lake, when visualized together, exemplify this carefully conceived region-wide systematic planning for water. You'll notice that the Sagar is organized at two levels. Once the upper reservoir fills up, catching the rain water runoff from the surrounding hills, excess water flows following gravity filling up the lower Sagar. The water then drips into the ground; recharging the water table and ultimately the step wells, water wells and other water bodies across the surrounding region. Serving a secondary function, Sagar also offers beautiful views of the surrounding hills and recreational opportunities for local residents and visiting tourists.

11. Akbari Mosque Raja Bharmal - 1569

Amer Road, Amer

Elegant building with some elements like the arches and wall panels belonging to local building traditions. When seen together with other influences of Mughal design ideas like the Aram Bagh and Diwan-i-aam, the Akbari mosque illustrates the processes of architectural synthesis that the contemporary builders were undertaking.

12. Bharmal ki Chhatri (Kachhawa Cenotaphs) Maharaja Sawai Jai Singh - 1575-80

Amer Road, Amer

Many communities in India practice open-air cremation, in which ashes (or *Asthies* in Hindi) are ritually dispersed, symbolizing humans' ultimately traceless return to nature. Highest ranking Rajput families, however, marked the spot of cremation via a chhatri or Cenotaph. Princely cremation ground relocated to *Gaitore* after Jaipur's development.

13. Hathi Gaon (Elephant Village) Ar. Rahul Mehrotra (RMA Architects) - 2010

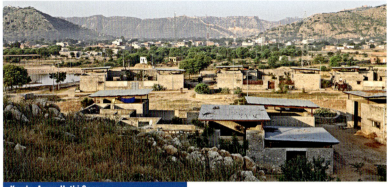
Kunda, Amer, Hathi Gaon

Site plan

Ground floor and first floor plans

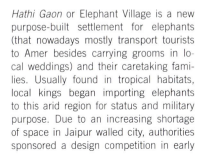

Hathi Gaon or Elephant Village is a new purpose-built settlement for elephants (that nowadays mostly transport tourists to Amer besides carrying grooms in local weddings) and their caretaking families. Usually found in tropical habitats, local kings began importing elephants to this arid region for status and military purpose. Due to an increasing shortage of space in Jaipur walled city, authorities sponsored a design competition in early 2000s. Apart from the unique social-living oriented cluster of housing units, targeting elephant comfort, the design approach's significance lies in a sensitive interpretation of the surrounding landscape centered upon catching and storing rainwater. Elephants prefer a water-rich environment and the overall planning pays careful attention to the topography, aiming to conserve every drop of rain water using purposeful landscape design strategies.

A. **Pearl Academy** Morphogenesis - 2008

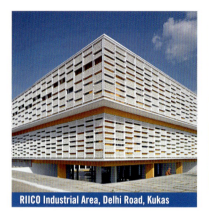

RIICO Industrial Area, Delhi Road, Kukas

Section

Underbelly Plan

India began liberalizing trade policies and loosening state control over key economic sectors like media from the 1990s. This catalyzed both a change in the country's overall approach to architecture as well as the rise of new building typologies like shopping malls, gated residential communities and private educational institutions. With foreign-trained architects and overseas-based design firms playing an increasingly important role, post-liberalization Indian architecture exhibits deep influences of contemporary global trends as well as a market-friendly orientation. Designed by a Delhi-based design firm, this campus is part of a nationwide private chain offering training in the fields of design, fashion and media. Oriented inwards toward an open atrium-like curvilinear space, the design pays attention to the harsh climate by employing a variety of thermal strategies like sunken areas, indoor waterbody and sun-breakers around external walls.

B. Lebua Lodge Amber Ar. P. Nath and A. Thanawala (Urban Studio) - 2013

Jaipur Kunda, NH-8 Tehsil, Amer

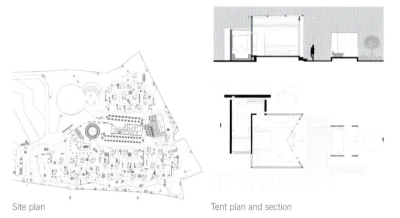

Site plan

Tent plan and section

Lebua Lodge is a visually stunning tourist resort designed by the young team of Mumbai based architects, Pronit Nath and Amisha Thanawala, trained in the U.K. The adopted design approach seeks to interpret the traditional tent for contemporary times; employing it as the basic living unit. Tents were routinely used by the royalty for camping and outdoor living during hunting and military expeditions in this part of the world. Beyond symbolic reference to spatial form,

the architects have also paid attention to the regional building practices as evident in the use of local elements like stone jaalis (or perforated stone screens / lattices) and prominent crafts such as hand-block printing used in the tent fabric. Although not open for general entry, visiting the resort restaurant for a snack or a lunch if possible, helps appreciate the tent's modern interpretation in the culturally appropriate settings of Amer.

Starting Point

Paanch Batti

1. Paanch Batti
2. Raj Mandir Cinema
3. MI Road
4. Ajmeri Gate
5. Museum of Legacies
   (Rajasthan School of Art)
6. Nataniyon Ki Haveli
7. Sargasuli Tower (or Isar lat)
8. Tripolia Bazaar
9. Tripolia Gate
10. Government Public Library
11. Shri Brijraj Bihariji Mandir
12. Badi Chaupad
13. Hawa Mahal
14. Sawai Man Singh Town Hall
15. Naqqar Khana and Sireh Deori Gates
16. Jaleb Chowk
17. Jantar Mantar
18. City Palace
    18.1 Diwan-i-Khaas
    18.2 Chandra Mahal
    18.3 Pritam Niwas Chowk
    18.4 Mubarak Mahal
    18.5 Baradari at City Palace Jaipur
19. Govind Dev Ji Temple
20. Jai Niwas Garden
21. Kale Hanuman Ji ka Mandir
22. Ram Prakash Theatre
23. Sireh Dehori Bazar
24. Shri Ram Chandraji Temple
25. Johari Bazaar
26. Sanganeri Gate
27. Bapu Bazaar
28. New Gate

zoom B

BERAVA
BASTI

BRAHMPURI
KHURRA

A PARK

GOVIND DEV
COLONY

⑳

㉑

㉒

PURANI BASTI

Brahmpuri Road

RAMCHA
CHAU

⑲

㉓

CHAND MAHAL
COLONY

ndpol Bazaar Road

Chhoti Chaupad

⑯

⑱

⑮

⑭ ㉔

CHANDPOL

⑰

⑦

⑥

⑧ ⑨

⑪

⑬

Kishanpol Bazaar Road

Maniharo Ka Rasta

⑩

⑫

Ramganj Bazaar Road

OPKHANA DESH

Chaura Rasta

JOHRI BAZAR

⑤

MODIKHANA

VIVESHWARJI

Johri Bazaar Road

ira Bazaar Road

④

FILM COLONY

GHAT
DARWAZA

㉕

Tonk Road

㉘

㉗

㉖

MI Road

Ram Niwas Bagh
Garden

Mahila Chikitsalaya

Rose Garden

0m   50m   200m   ↑ N

43

zoom A

Tivari ji Haveli

Chandpol Bazaar Road

Shri Roof Charbhuja Mandir
Shri Charbhuja Mandir

C H A N D P O L

Mahaveer
Rabdi Bhandar
Bhojanalaya

Kotwali
Police Station

Shree Prajeet
Chat Bhandar

W O O D   C A R V I N G

Sammpat
Namkeen
Bhandar

Nataniyon Ki
Haveli 6

Jhalaniyon Ka Rasta

Khajane Walon Ka Rasta

M A R B E L   C A R V I N G

Bh.
Mis
Bhar

Pandey
Moorti Kala Kendra

Khutela
Namkeen Bhandar

Museum
Legacies

5

Kishanpol Bazaar Road

Pandi
Shivdeen j
Haveli

M

Indira Bazaar Road

4 Ajmeri Gate

Yadgar
(Clock Tower)

A

Nayika

Gem Palace

Indian
Coffee House

Lassi Wala

Tholia Building

Amrapali Jewels

3
MI Road

Rajasthan Handicraft
Emporium

Panch
Batti 1

Nataraj

Niros

Surya Mahal

2

Rajmandir Cinema

Ram N

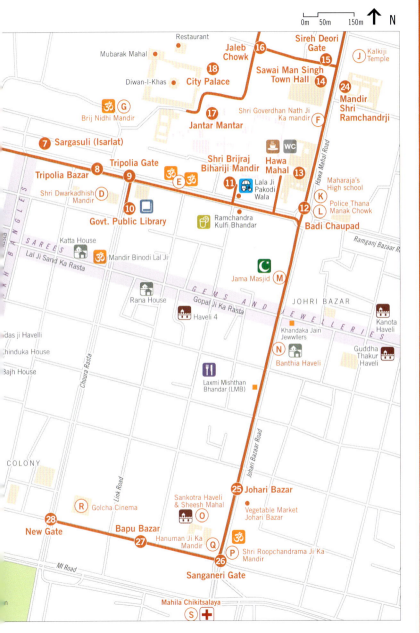

0m 50m 150m ↑ N

Restaurant
Mubarak Mahal
Jaleb Chowk
Sireh Deori Gate
16
J Kalkiji Temple
18
15
City Palace
Diwan-I-Khas
Sawai Man Singh Town Hall
14
24
Mandir Shri Ramchandrji
G Brij Nidhi Mandir
17
Jantar Mantar
Shri Goverdhan Nath Ji Ka mandir
F
7 Sargasuli (Isarlat)
Hawa Mahal Road
8 Tripolia Gate
Shri Brijraj Bihariji Mandir
WC
Tripolia Bazar
9
E
Hawa Mahal
13
Shri Dwarkadhish Mandir
D
11 Lala Ji Pakodi Wala
Maharaja's High school
K
10
Govt. Public Library
Ramchandra Kulfi Bhandar
12
L Police Thana Manak Chowk
Badi Chaupad
Ramganj Bazaar R
SAREES
Katta House
Lal Ji Sand Ka Rasta
Mandir Binodi Lal Ji
BANGLES
KH
Jama Masjid
M
JOHRI BAZAR
Rana House
GEMS AND
Gopal Ji Ka Rasta
Haveli 4
JEWELLERIES
Kanota Haveli
das ji Havelli
hinduka House
Khandaka Jain Jewwllers
Guddha Thakur Haveli
N
Bajh House
Banthia Haveli
Choura Rasta
Laxmi Mishthan Bhandar (LMB)
COLONY
Link Road
25 Johari Bazar
Johari Bazaar Road
R Golcha Cinema
Sankotra Haveli & Sheesh Mahal
O
Vegetable Market Johari Bazar
28
Bapu Bazar
New Gate
Hanuman Ji Ka Mandir
Q
P Shri Roopchandrama Ji Ka Mandir
27
26
MI Road
Sanganeri Gate
Mahila Chikitsalaya
S ✚

45

Additional buildings:

A. Yaadgar
B. Chhoti Chaupad and Flowers Market
C. Shri Chaturbhuj ka Mandir and Shri Roop
   Chaturbhuj ka Mandir
D. Shri Dwarkadheesh Mandir
E. Tripolia Bazaar Temples
F. Govardhan Nath Ji Ka Mandir
G. Brij Nidhi Mandir
H. Tal Katora
I. Shri Girdhariji Ka Mandir
J. Kalkiji Mandir
K. Maharaja High School
L. Police Station Thana Manak Chowk
M. Jama Masjid
N. Banthia Haveli
O. Sankotra Haveli and Sheesh Mahal
P. Shri Roopchandrama Ji Ka Mandir
Q. Sanganeri Gate Hanuman Ji Temple
R. Golcha Cinema
S. Mahila Chikitsalaya (Hospital)

Restaurants:

Baradari, Restaurant and Bar
City Palace
Grand Chanakya, Leisure Inn Grand
Chanakya Hotel, Paanch Batti, MI Road
www.leisureinngrandchanakya.in
Laxmi Mishthan Bhandar (LMB Hotel)
No. 98-101, Johari Bazaar
Natraj, Paanch Batti, MI Road
Niros, Paanch Batti, MI Road
www.nirosindia.com
Surya Mahal, Paanch Batti, MI Road
www.suryamahal.com

Sweet Shops and Ice Cream Parlors:
Bhagat Mishthan Bhandar
Galundia Bhavan, Opp. Aakashvani, MI Road,
Sindhi Camp
www.bhagatmishthan.com
Lassiwala Kishanlal Govind Narayan
Agarwal, Paanch Batti, MI Road
Vijay Stores, No 245-246, Kishanpole Bazaar

Shopping:

Amrapali Jewels, Paanch Batti, MI Road
www.amrapalijewels.com
Gem Palace, No 348, MI Road
www.gempalace.com
Khandaka Jain Jewellers, 3-4-5, Haldiyon Ka
Raasta, Johari Bazaar
Nayika (Clothing and Home Furnishing),
Tholia Building, MI Road
www.nayika-jaipur.com
Rajasthali Handicraft Emporium, Opposite
Ajmeri Gate, MI Road
www.rajasthancrafts.gov.in

zoom B

0m 50m 150m   N

BRAHMPURI
KHURRA

Gangori Bazar Marg

Rajamal ka Talab Road

(H) **Talkatora**

Shri Girdhariji
Ka Mandir (I)

GOVIND DEV
COLONY

(20)
Jai Niwas Garden

Kale Hanumanji Ka (21)
Mandir

**Shri Govind Devji
Mandir**

**Ram Prakash
Theatre** (22)

(19)

**Sireh Deori
Bazar** (23)

CHAND MAHAL
COLONY

Baradari
The Palace Cafe
Restaurant

**Sireh Deori
Gate**

Mubarak Mahal

**Jaleb
Chowk** (16)

(15)

(J) Kalkiji
Temple

**Sawai Man Singh
Town Hall** (14)

(18)

Diwan-I-Khas

City Palace

(24)
**Mandir
Shri
Ramchandrji**

(17)
Jantar Mantar

Shri Goverdhan Nath Ji
Ka mandir (F)

(G)
Brij Nidhi Mandir

(7) **Sargasuli (Isarlat)**

**Shri Brijraj
Bihariji Mandir**

**Hawa
Mahal**

WC

Tripolia Gate

(13)

Hawa Mahal Road

(8)

Tripolia Bazar

(9)

(E)

(11) Lala Ji
Pakodi
Wala

Maharaja's
High school

**Shri Dwarkadhish
Mandir** (D)

(K)

(10)

Govt. Public Library

Ramchandra
Kulfi Bhandar

(12)

Police Thana
Manak Chowk (L)

Badi Chaupad

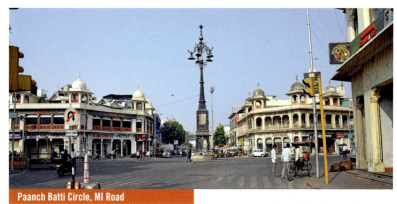

Paanch Batti Circle, MI Road

ITINERARY II **THE WALLED CITY**

ITINERARY LEVEL: Medium (by foot)
DURATION: more than one day
DISTANCE: around 2 km

DRONAH Foundation Heritage Walk:
'Chowkri Modikhana Heritage Walk'
www.dronahfoundation.org/heritage-walk/

PRACTICAL INFORMATION:

The City Palace, Jantar Mantar, Hawa
Mahal and major monuments are open
to the public. There is an entry fee, see
'Monuments Timings' p. 210.

Most of the city temples are open to the
public from early morning till evening.

Unfortunately most of the havelis and
private propieties are not open to the public
but no harm asking.

This itinerary travels a bit along the Mirza Ismail (MI) road before exploring part of the
walled city and the main seat of princely
power, popularly called the 'city palace.'
Must do itinerary, especially if short on time,
because it gives you a firsthand feel of the
three main architectural influences that
shaped Jaipur over a period of around two
centuries, from the founding in year 1727 to
the early 20th century. The first set of influences center around regionally developed
practices, visible in the widespread use of
characteristic features like arches, domes,
jaalis, and chhatris, variants of which are
also found in nearby places like Shekhawati,
Jodhpur and Udaipur.

The second influence came via political
collaborations and cultural exchanges with
the powerful Mughal empire (India's ruling dynasty of Turkish-Mongol origin headquartered a short distance away at Delhi
and Agra) and is perhaps best evident in

Aerial view of Chandpol and the Tripolia Bazaars

the use of design elements like the symmetrical four-quadrant gardens (or the so-called *Char Bagh*) and typologies like the diwan-i-khaas, explained a little later.

The third set of influences came with the ascendancy of British Raj and stands out due to its striking contrast with the two older traditions. For example, notice the use of faux pediments and Romanesque columns at the Sawai Man Singh Town Hall and Government Public Library. In this sense, there

is neither a 'classical style' nor a 'pure type' of Jaipur architecture. But the city's overall architecture illustrates an eclectically rich mix of diverse building elements and design features that the city's many builders, belonging to different generations and backgrounds, freely experimented with, and frequently mixed, per their own aspirations and preferences, collectively creating a unique Indian city—unmatched anywhere else in the entire subcontinent.

1. **Paanch Batti** Maharaja Sawai Man Singh II - 1930

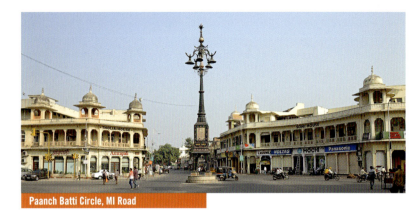

Paanch Batti Circle, MI Road

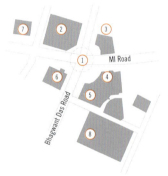

MI Road

Bhagwant Das Road

Site plan

1. Paanch Batti Circle
2. Barbeque Nation Restaurant
3. Amrapali Jewels
4. J&k Bank
5. Mc Donald's
6. Gramya Khadi Handicraft Emporium
7. Gas Station
8. Raj Mandir Cinema

The phrase *Paanch Batti* literally means five lights. Notice the prominent light mast, located at the center of this busy intersection, that comprises five lamps symbolizing the name. The architectural and spatial planning importance of this place, however, transcends the simple name. The 'New colony,' Jaipur's first planned expansion outside the city wall, developed in the 1930s, is located just north of this intersection. Just South is the most affluent of the five major city-extensions called C Scheme developed in the late 1940s while the well-known M.I. road along the East-West axis was developed in the early 1940s. So, this intersection embodies the meeting point of the three major city-expansion projects that the princely authorities sponsored just before seceding power to the post-independence Indian state. The four curved buildings around Paanch Batti use signature elements like arches and chhatris and, emphasizing the roundabout's curvature, are built up to the property line.

2. Raj Mandir Cinema Ar W.M. Namjoshi - 1976

Paanch Batti, Bhagwant Das Road

Ground floor plan

First floor plan

Located close to the Paanch Batti intersection, Raj Mandir cinema is a local landmark attracting both city residents and visiting tourists, due to its attractive interiors purposefully designed in an opulent manner. Sponsored by a prominent Jaipur family involved in jewelry trade and real-estate development, Raj Mandir aims to represent city's princely past via a lavish interpretation of the late 'Art deco' movement. Designed by Bombay-based architect W.M. Namjoshi, who was clearly inspired by the Art deco style employed in British Bombay during the early 20th century—especially in cinema halls like the Regal—Raj Mandir's double-height circular lobby, the movie hall and the overall internal environment including the carpets, false ceiling, chandeliers, elevational treatment, murals and the exuberant colors of the walls showcase careful detailing and close supervision. The Raj Mandir cinema took almost 10 years to complete and quickly gained prominence after its opening in 1976.

3. MI Road (Mirza Ismail Road) Maharaja Sawai Man Singh II - XXth Cent.

MI Road

Mirza Ismail, Jaipur's progressive prime-minister for a short period in the early 1940s, sponsored the building of M.I. Road, later named in his memory. Conceived as an arterial road fronting upscale shopping stores, the overall architecture of this place exhibits close similarities with contemporary developments in British India.

4. Ajmeri Gate (Kishanpol Gate) Maharaja Sawai Jai Singh

Nehru Bazaar Road, Modikhana

Ajmeri Gate is one of the seven similarly-designed gates into the walled city. Strategically located, Ajmeri Gate takes its name from the old route linking Jaipur to the city of Ajmer. Recently refurbished, Ajmeri Gate has retained its public significance as an important landmark.

5. Museum of Legacies (formerly Rajasthan School of Art) - 1866

Kishanpol Bazaar Rd, Modikhana

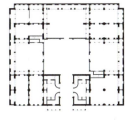

Elevation and ground floor plan

Notwithstanding changes of name and function from the original *Madrasa-i-Hunari* to the Maharaja School of Art to the recent repurposing as an elegantly conceptualized 'Museum of Legacies,' this place signifies the maiden attempt to establish a modern art school dedicated to teaching traditional crafts in a formalized studio-workshop environment at Jaipur. With the steady advent of colonial influences in all walks of indigenous life, progressive British officials and local elites feared the loss of 'oriental' skills. Following the successful establishment of JJ schools of Arts in Bombay around the mid 19th century, several princely states like Baroda and Jaipur followed suit. The building design itself is fairly simple: A square plan centered around a courtyard adjoining a variety of rooms all-around. The front elevation centered upon a prominent entrance gate, or *Pol*, reflects the symmetrical simplicity.

6. **Nataniyon Ki Haveli** Maharaja Sawai Jai Singh II - 1870-1880

Kishanpol Bazaar Road, Chandpol

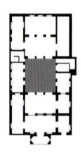 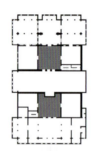 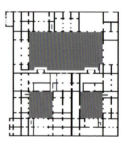

Representative plans for havelis with different number of courtyards

Nataniyon *Ki Haveli* simply means the mansion of the Natani family. Natani is a sub-group of locally prominent merchants and traders called the *Khandelwals*. As evident in the sheer physical size and grand elevation, a wealthy and well-connected patron sponsored the building of this Haveli—one of the best exemplars of this type in Jaipur. Havelis constituted the basic residential type in this climatically arid part of the World stretching from the Middle-east to Northwest India. Essentially inward-oriented buildings comprising one-or-several open-to-sky courtyards, depending upon the plot size and sponsors' wealth (this one, for instance, comprises seven courtyards), and a variety of different sized rooms, their spatial layout offered easy adaptation to diverse needs and changing requirements. This Haveli, for example, was taken over by the state and converted partly into a major police station and a government school. Recently, it has been recognized as a 'protected monument' by the state authorities.

7. Sargasuli or Isar lat Raja Ishwari Singh - 1749

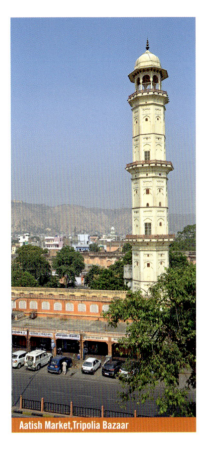

Aatish Market,Tripolia Bazaar

Elevation

Sargasuli means stairway to heaven, while the phrase Isar lat (another equally popular name for this building) translates as Ishwar's tower. Built by Sawai Ishwari Singh, Jaipur's second king who succeeded the founder Sawai Jai Singh, this building is one of the tallest free-standing structures in the walled city. Historians report no specific purpose for its building, but the local folklore offers a couple of plausible stories in addition to a simple royal whim. One anecdote describes the purported commemoration of a grand war victory and the second illustrates a secretive tale of love. Sawai Ishwari Singh apparently fell for a pretty girl who lived opposite this tower. Unfortunately, her father was his prime minister, a gentleman called Hargobind Natani, and prevalent caste restrictions and social protocols precluded any kind of formal interaction. Thus, only way the King could steal a glance was by building a tall tower like the Isar Lat.

8. **Tripolia Bazaar** Maharaja Sawai Jai Singh II - 1734

Tripolia Bazaar, Badi Chaupad

Tripolia Bazaar portico

Adjoining the Tripolia Gate, this Bazaar mainly caters to city residents. Recognizing the importance of trade and commerce, Jaipur Maharajas sponsored a variety of bazaars along all the major thoroughfares of the city. Not a fancy or upscale place like the Johri Bazaar, Tripolia bazaar houses diverse shops, such as those selling utensils, groceries and ready to eat food items, and therefore offers an excellent slice of local city life to the visiting tourists.

Tripolia Bazaar on reaching Chhoti Chaupad

9. Tripolia Gate Maharaja Sawai Jai Singh II - 1734

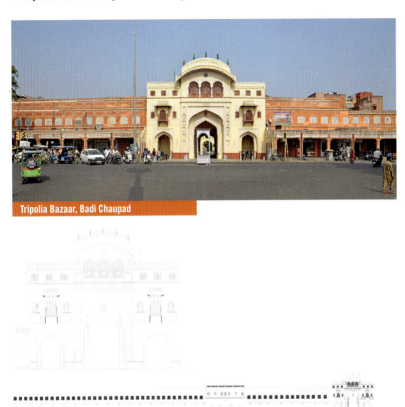

Tripolia Bazaar, Badi Chaupad

Tripolia Bazaar (and gate) elevation

Tripolia means three doorways. True to the straightforward name, Tripolia comprises three gates; with two small ones flanking the bigger doorway that aligns axially with the symmetrical center of the overall structure housing the beautifully decorated ceremonial entrance into the city place complex. Located at a 'T' junction, Tripolia also constitutes one of the city's more important intersections with outward roads leading to the Badi and Chhoti Chaupad, walled city's iconic public spaces, and Jaipur's later expansion beyond the circumferential wall via the Ajmeri gate. It is important to note that, apart from the exclusive use by the members of royal household that still owns and controls this property, Tripolia serves important public functions such as the launch of celebratory processions marking the locally popular Teej and Gangaur festivals. In this sense, Tripolia serves more as an engaging backdrop to a lively civic space than a mere doorway delineating private and public realms.

Tripolia Bazaar Elevation

Chhoti Chaupad

Tripolia Gate

10. Government Public Library Maharaja Sawai Ram Singh II

Chaura Rasta Road

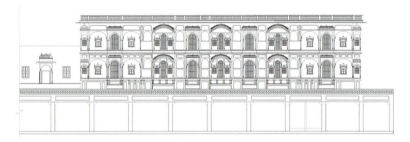

Elevation (Tripolia Bazaar)

This building houses the first-ever public library constructed in the entire Jaipur region. Unfortunately, not in good condition presently, so perhaps best not to spend too much time inside the library but to appreciate the external form standing outside. Notice how the building's front elevation combines elements from the colonial palette on the upper floors such as the raised columns and faux pediments, further highlighted using a different color, along with a traditional doorway resembling that of a grand Haveli. The uneasy effort to combine two different building traditions not only represents the strenuous adoption of imported features into Jaipur's spatial form but also signifies the builder's quest for an appropriate architectural vocabulary befitting the new civic function of a public library. Historically, only the well-to-do received an education and could read. But a public library, by its very nature, welcomes everyone, demanding a new kind of architecture.

11. Shri Brijraj Bihariji Mandir Maharaja Sawai Pratap Singh

Tripolia Bazaar, J.D.A. Market

Hindusim comprises two major sects of Shaivism, devoted to Shiva, and Vaishnavism, those considering Vishnu and his avatars, such as Rama and Krishna, the supreme lord. Most of the Jaipur's ruling dynasty subscribed to Vaishnavism sponsoring temples dedicated to Bhagwan Krishna. Brijraj Bihari temple is a magnificent courtyard-based temple, fashioned as a Haveli, exemplifying the devotion of its builders.

12. Badi Chaupad Maharaja Sawai Jai Singh II/Ram Singh II - 1874

Badi Chaupad

Badi means large and Chaupad, in this context, means open public space. Fashioned like a grand plaza with carefully designed corner spaces called the Khandas, Badi Chaupad serves like a public hub attracting travelers, residents, hawkers, itinerant vendors and specialized markets. Owing to the central location and flexible nature, this open space has been adapted to a variety of functional uses over time. Ongoing plans, for instance, envisage an underground metro station in this area.

13. **Hawa Mahal** Maharaja Sawai Pratap Singh - 1799

Hawa Mahal Road, Badi Chaupad

Section

Hawa Mahal literally means the palace of wind. This is certainly a signature building, dominating web searches on Jaipur and featuring on picture postcards and promotional posters published by the provincial and national tourism agencies. Typically, a must-visit place for every tourist. However, Hawa Mahal is actually less of a usable building and more of a painstakingly conceptualized façade, lower parts of which provide frontage to a few rooms and open-to-sky court-yards at the rear, while the upper floors are just about a few feet in depth. The overall elevation, however, is playfully composed combining a diverse range of architectural elements and fenestrations including windows, brackets, screens and arches. Sponsored by Sawai Pratap Singh, Jaipur's third King who, rather curiously, did not undertake any other notable building work during his reign, Hawa Mahal was a deeply cultural project dedicated to the royal ladies.

Open-to-sky courtyard views

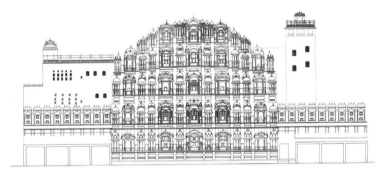

Elevati

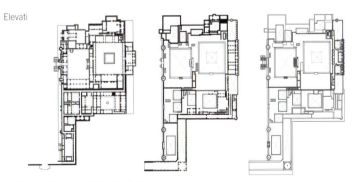

Ground, Second and Fourth plans

14. Sawai Man Singh Town Hall Maharaja Ram Singh II / Sawai Madho Singh II - 1884

Hawa Mahal Road (Sireh Deori Bazaar)

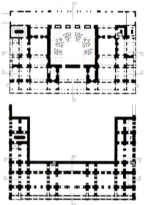

Plans (lower level and ground floor)

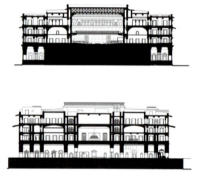

Sections

Sawai Man Singh Town Hall's spatial form and social purpose symbolizes the new kind of civic architecture inspired by European influences that came into play during Sawai Ram Singh's reign (1835-1880). Designed by the prolific engineer Swinton Jacob, it was originally conceived to house the Jaipur Exhibition in 1883. Following the 'Great Exhibition,' sometimes also called as the 'crystal palace exhibition,' organized at London in 1851, the idea of showcasing latest geographic explorations, scientific knowledges, and industrial advancements to the general public had gained currency across the British empire. The Town Hall comprises a series of different sized halls and, given the flexible nature of internal layout, was put to a variety of uses after the exhibition. For instance, it served as a venue for the princely state's official functions, subsequently housed the Rajasthan state's legislative assembly in the post-independence period, and is presently slated for repurposing as a public Museum.

15. Naqqar Khana and Sireh Deori Gates Maharaja Sawai Jai Singh II

Hawa Mahal Road (Sireh Deori Bazaar)

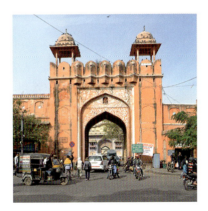

Naqqar Khana Gate

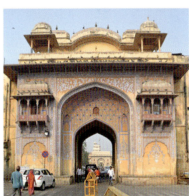

Sireh Deori Gate

Located close to Hawa Mahal, these adjacent places mark the City Palace's second entrance. While Tripolia gate was intended for ceremonial functions, this entrance served everyday purposes. Denoting the border between the royal premises and commoners' domain, their collective socio-spatial importance, however, can be gauged by their imposing presence and the adjoining markets that derive their names from these entrances viz Tripolia Bazaar and Sireh Deori Bazaar. Here, it is important to note that

Jaipur kings, like many elsewhere, were perceived by many subjects as descendants of the Sun god—a myth that the kings and their courtiers supported in self-interest through pompous rituals and elaborate protocol. *Naqqar Khana*, meaning the drum house, was such a supportive feature borrowed from the Mughal traditions that housed musicians playing instruments to announce the royal threshold while *Sireh Deori* literally means the boundary gate which leads the visitor into the impressive Jaleb chowk.

16. Jaleb Chowk Maharaja Sawai Jai Singh - 1693-1743

Jaleb Chowk, Tulsi Marg

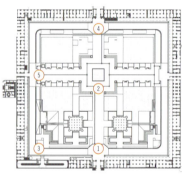

1. Sireh Deori Gate
2. Tulsi Marg
3. Town Hall entrance, formely
4. City Palace entrance
5. To Jantar Mantar

Ground floor plan

Enclosed by perimeter buildings, Jaleb chowk is an open-to-sky space providing access to other areas like Jantar-Mantar and the royal palace. It served multiple functions including the royal court's interface with its subjects because most commoners were simply not allowed to proceed beyond this place. The design typology itself is not new, having been previously used in the Amer fort, but the scale and composition are certainly impressive, befitting a new capital city. The royal court used this sizable space to interact with the general public in a variety of ways like cavalry display and military drills showcasing state power, and for housing administrative office requiring frequent interaction with the commoners. In the post-independence period, the newly formed state of Rajasthan commandeered Jaleb chowk to house the many government offices that a modern bureaucracy requires. Plans to redevelop this area as an Arts Complex have been under discussion for some time now.

17. **Jantar Mantar** Maharaja Sawai Jai Singh II - 1738

Jaleb Chowk, Chowkri Sarhad

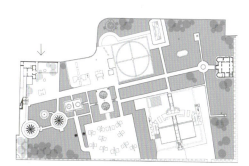

Site plan

Jantar Mantar means 'black magic' in colloquial parlance. At some level, the choice of this phrase for the observatory Jaipur's founder-king built for housing his architectural astronomical devices echoes the popular sentiment toward unfamiliar abstract ideas. On the other hand, Jai Singh's building of similar observatories in other places like Delhi illustrates how progressive Indian elites were not only striving to keep abreast with contemporary scientific advancements but were also not afraid of experimenting on their own in larger public settings. Reportedly, Jai Singh's pursuits in the field of astronomy even involved exchanges with Portuguese and Chinese scholars. In this respect, the phenomena also signified the many transnational linkages Jaipur rulers fostered with the wider world that ultimately supported city's outward-oriented economic focus as evident, for example, in the jewelry business and tourism industry.

18. **City Palace** Maharaja Sawai Jai Singh, Vidyadhar Bhattacharya - 1729-1732

City Palace Complex

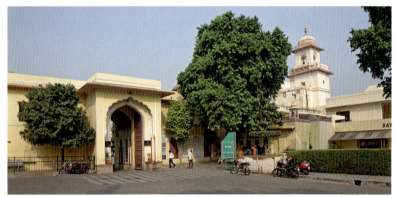

City Palace complex entrance and aerial views of Diwan-i-Khaas's open-to-the-sky courtyard

The city palace complex is situated at the very heart of Jaipur—occupying two entire squares out of the total nine that make up the whole city—illustrating the king's political power and social standing via his palace's geographical location and physical spread. In terms of spatial layout and organization, the palace can be both visualized as a self-contained city within a city and also as a diligent combination of diverse land uses and buildings serving the royalty's many personal needs and functional demands involving life, work and play. In terms of design, the palace complex represents the collective work of several kings promoting different practices over couple centuries. Thus, the complex's overall architecture comprises an assortment of built, semi-open, and open spaces including a substantial water body. In addition to the Jaleb chowk and Govind Dev ji temple described separately, some of the more important building are described next.

18.1 **Diwan-i-Khaas** Vidyadhar Bhattacharya - 1729-1732

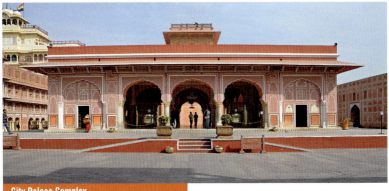

City Palace Complex

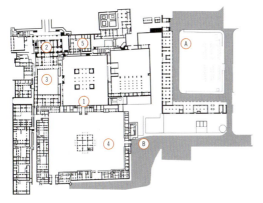

A. Jaleb Chowk
B. Entrance
1. Diwan-i-Khaas
2. Chandra Mahal
3. Pritam Niwas Chowk
4. Mubarak Mahal
5. Baradari at City Palace Jaipur

Site plan

The phrase *diwan-i-khaas* means 'the hall of private audience (typically with important visitors).' Essentially a richly decorated hall, located close to the Mubarak Mahal that served as a welcoming center, this place provided a private venue for the Maharaja to meet high-ranking visitors. The typology of diwan-i-khaas came to Jaipur via the influence of Mughal architecture with excellent examples evident in the red forts of Delhi and Agra. It serves as an art gallery today.

Although no biography or detailed life account exists, Vidhyadhar Bhattacharya is popularly credited as the conceiver of Jaipur's city plan. Born into a Brahmin household, employed as the priests of a locally-prominent temple in Amer fort, Vidhyadhar reportedly demonstrated an abiding interest in building work from an early age. Noticed by the royal court, he moved up the professional ladder designing progressively important projects culminating with the founding plan for the entire city.

18.2 Chandra Mahal (Zenana Deodhi) Vidyadhar Bhattacharya - 1729-1732

The dinning area on ground floor, and the blue room called Sukh Niwas at 2nd floor (below)

Interiors of the Chandra Mahal palace

Comprising seven floors, Chandra Mahal is a rather imposing building sited among carefully conceived landscaped areas. Each floor is named individually and designed and decorated lavishly in line with the designated use as well. While the upper floors are still used as the primary residence of Maharaja's descendants, the ground floor now serves as a museum open to tourists. A beautiful gate adorned with peacock reliefs marks Chandra Mahal's entrance.

Entrance gate to Pritam Niwas Chowk from Diwan-i-Khaas

18.3 Pritam Niwas Chowk

City Palace Complex

Site plan

Pritam Niwas means the 'home of the beloved.' Framed by theme-based elaborately-decorated entrance gates, this is one of the more carefully designed courtyards providing access to royalty's private quarters. Used for a variety of celebratory events and royal entertainments, this courtyard provided an open-to-sky venue for the many residents, especially the women, who spent much of their life sequestered within the palace complex.

Leheriya Gate

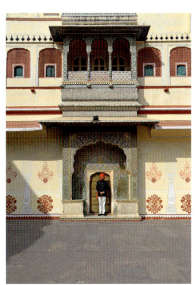

Rose Gate

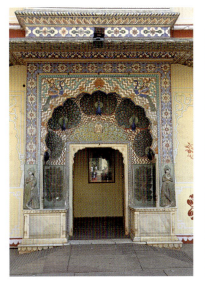

Peacock Gate

Lotus Gate

18.4 Mubarak Mahal Maharaja Sawai Madho Singh II

City Palace Complex

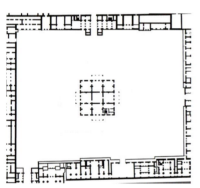

Ground floor plan. On right, detail of the Udai Pol, one of the gates into palace complex

Built in the late 19th century, and thus among the last few additions to the complex, Mubarak Mahal was designed to receive important state guests. Accordingly, not only is this building situated close to the entrance into the palace complex but also built to impress. Using an eclectic mix of highly-ornamental elevational features from diverse architectural traditions, Mubarak Mahal now serves as a museum showcasing some of its creator's impressive belongings.

18.5 Baradari at City Palace Jaipur Studio Lotus - 2016

City Palace Complex

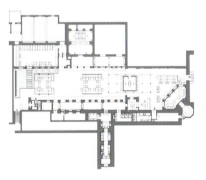

Site plan

Section

Successive kings routinely adopted buildings and places in line with personal preferences and changing requirements. Baradari, a recently commissioned eating placc comprising a bar, lounge, open-seating restaurant and private dining, is one of the latest such changes. With the abolition of princely rule and the cessation of traditional incomes, many erstwhile rulers and their descendants turned towards tourism industry as it fitted well with their sizeable property portfolio, renowned hospitality, and the overall Rajput culture of generosity. In fact, Jaipur royal family was a pioneer taking lead with the conversion of Ram Bagh palace into a super-luxury heritage hotel (see itinerary 06 for details). Baradari, overseen by the entrepreneurial Princess Diya Kumari—the only offspring of present titular queen Padmini Devi and last Maharaja Brigadier Bhawani Singh ji—who takes active interest in managing the royal properties, owes its charm to the romantic location and careful repurposing.

19. Govind Dev Ji Temple Maharaja Sawai Pratap Singh II - 1735

Jai Niwas Gardens, Jaleb Chowk

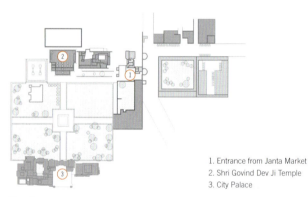

Site plan

1. Entrance from Janta Market
2. Shri Govind Dev Ji Temple
3. City Palace

One of the most popular shrines in the entire Jaipur city, this temple is known simply by the presiding deity—Govind Dev Ji, one of the several names for Bhagwan Krishna. Various legends describe the idol's mythical origins, many travels, and eventual installation at the present location. But perhaps most importantly, built and patronized by the founder-king himself, who was an avowed devotee of Krishna per familial traditions, the simple and no-frills temple is not only sited in direct line of sight from the Chandra Mahal but ostensibly also from the King's own bedroom. It, thus, occupies a special place both in the palace's geography and city's religious life. This comes clear in the robust congregation that takes place seven times daily, with each session typically lasting around 30-45 minutes, when personal devotion scales up to an impressive collective expression energizing the public space of temple's forecourt. A must visit.

20. **Jai Niwas Garden** Maharaja Sawai Pratap Singh - 1868

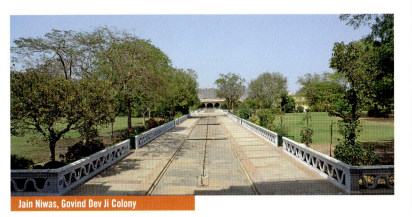
Jain Niwas, Govind Dev Ji Colony

Located in close proximity to Govind Dev Ji, the garden's layout is in line with the then-popular Mughal Char Bagh pattern. When seen in conjunction with the nearby Tal Katora lake and the Chaugan stadium, it formed part of the outdoor-oriented recreational facilities available within walking distance from the royal quarters.

21. **Kale Hanuman Ji Ka Mandir** - 9th Cent.

Amer Road, Janta Market

Bhagwan, or lord, Hanuman is widely perceived as both easy-to-please and giver of strength and fearlessness. Legend holds that this shrine precedes the building of Jaipur and, unlike other temples where the idol is customarily orange or red in color, here he is *Kale*, or black, and the hence the temple's name.

22. Ram Prakash Theatre Maharaja Ram Singh II - 1878

Sireh Deori Bazaar, Chandi ki Taksal

This is the first theatre anywhere in this region built by Sawai Ram Singh, who pursued diverse hobbies including the newly-introduced craft of photography and sponsored the building of this theatre, as the city lacked recreational opportunities beyond the traditional ones. He routinely invited theatre groups and touring companies from other cities.

23. Sireh Deori Bazaar Maharaja Sawai Jai Singh II

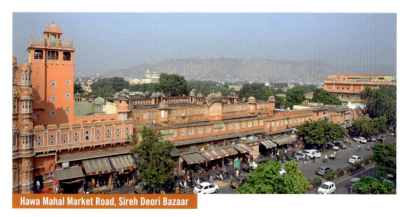

Hawa Mahal Market Road, Sireh Deori Bazaar

One of the several main bazars envisaged in the city's founding plan to support and promote Jaipur's economic base, the Sireh Deori bazaar is situated alongside and opposite the Hawa Mahal. Given the steady tourist flow through this area, the bazar now mainly caters visiting tourists offering opportunities to shop as they tour the landmark.

24. Shri Ram Chandraji Temple Maharaja Sawai Jagat Singh

Sireh Deohri Bazaar, opp. Town Hall

Ground floor plan

Elevation

Located in the Sireh Deori Bazaar, on the touristic route to-and-fro from Hawa Mahal, this is an elaborate temple with a magnificent entrance gate. The building footprint covers almost an acre of land and the functional space is organized around nine courtyards—plausibly echoing the layout of the city itself. Motivated by a favorite queen, Sawai Jagat Singh sponsored the building of this temple around the middle of the nineteenth century. Fashioned almost along the lines of a princely palace, and thus befitting the status of a royal's chosen deity, the temple's architectural elements combine a range of Jaipur's trademark features like arches, brackets, carved pillars and domical roofs. Hindu tradition holds that idols are living personification of heavenly gods, and this belief leads to their caretaking as actual persons. Multiple ceremonies, therefore, celebrate the deities' everyday routines offering frequent opportunities to participate in prayers and accompanying rituals.

25. Johari Bazaar Maharaja Sawai Jai Singh II

Johari Bazaar

The central location of Johari bazaar, or the Jeweler's market, denotes the importance royal court accorded to this activity, essentially signifying a prosperous city. However, Jaipur neither produces raw materials nor consumes much of the end-products but specializes in polishing gemstones, manufacturing jewelry and importing/exporting across the world.

26. Sanganeri Gate Maharaja Sawai Jai Singh II

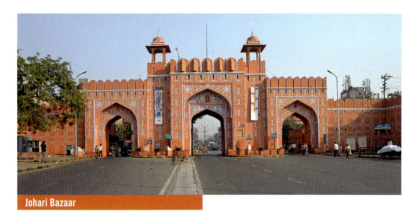

Johari Bazaar

One of the seven gates into the walled city, Sanganeri gate links the well-known *Johari Bazaar,* or the Jeweler's market, with the important satellite town of Sanganer, famous for the fabric, popularly called 'Sanganeri print,' made with traditional hand-block printing technique. The locally popular Hanuman temple is located just north of Sanganeri gate .

27. Bapu Bazaar

Bapu Bazaar

Bapu Bazaar is a later addition (1950s) to the city plan; developed to house (mainly) Sindhi migrants who moved to Jaipur from the adjacent province of Sindh (Pakistan) following the partition of British India. Specializing in a diverse range of goods, souvenirs and gifts, it is one of the busiest markets in the entire city.

28. New Gate Maharaja Sawai Man Singh II - 1940

Choura Rasta, Nehru Bazaar

The gate links Tripolia gate to MI Road. Originally built as a small gate (ostensibly due to the strictures of *Vastu Shastra* or Sanskrit treatises describing city planning and building principals), its conversion into the present form enabled quick access to outlying areas resulting from Jaipur's outward-oriented development in the early 20th century.

ADDITIONAL BUILDINGS

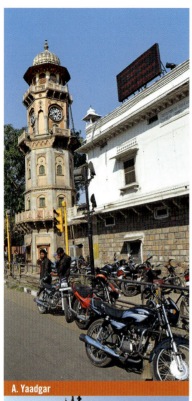

A. Yaadgar

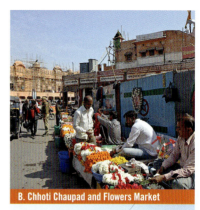

B. Chhoti Chaupad and Flowers Market

C. Shri Roop Chaturbhuj ka Mandir

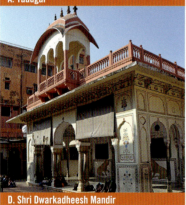

D. Shri Dwarkadheesh Mandir

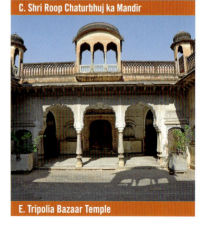

E. Tripolia Bazaar Temple

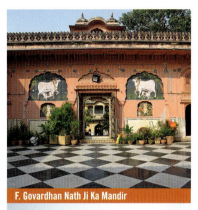

F. Govardhan Nath Ji Ka Mandir

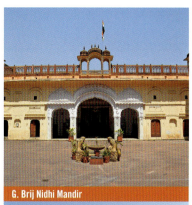

G. Brij Nidhi Mandir

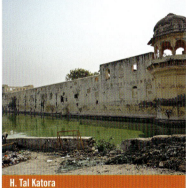

H. Tal Katora

I. Shri Girdhariji ka Mandir

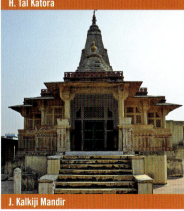

J. Kalkiji Mandir

K. Maharaja High School

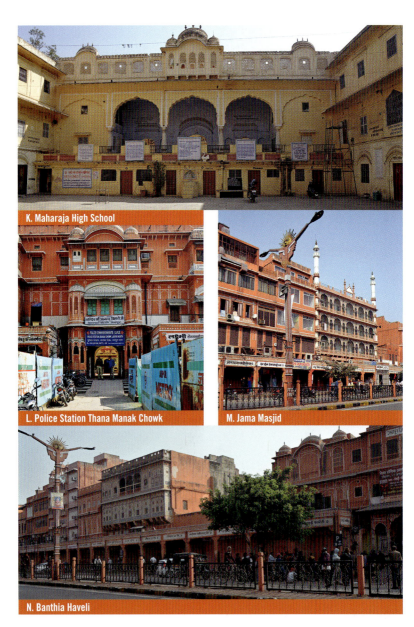

K. Maharaja High School

L. Police Station Thana Manak Chowk

M. Jama Masjid

N. Banthia Haveli

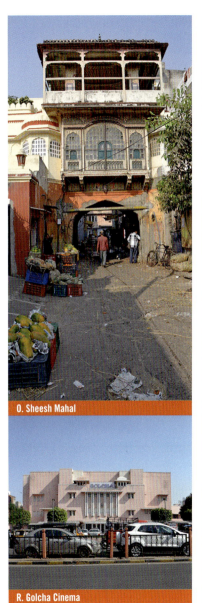

O. Sheesh Mahal

R. Golcha Cinema

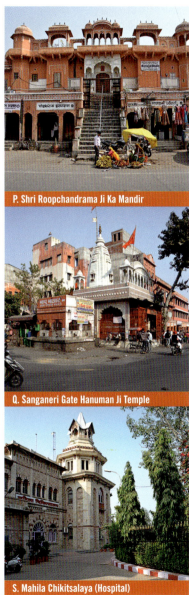

P. Shri Roopchandrama Ji Ka Mandir

Q. Sanganeri Gate Hanuman Ji Temple

S. Mahila Chikitsalaya (Hospital)

Purani Basti Chowkdi (ZOOM A)
Gangauri Bazaar
Nahargarh Rd **(Wooden Hand Blocks)**
Tivari ji Haveli
Lal Hathi ka Mandir
Khothari ji ki Haveli
Purani Basti Raasta
Khawas ji Mandir
Radha Gopinath Mandir
Khatu Haveli Hotel
Balanand ji ka Mandir
Shree Ram Chandra Ji
Chandpol Darwaza

Chandpol Bazaar & Topkhana Desh Chowkdi
(ZOOM A)
Chandpol Bazaar
Mahaveer Rabdi Bhandar Bhojanalaya
(Eatery-Sweets)
Shree Prajeet Chat Bhandar **(Eatery-Snacks)**
Sammpat Namkeen Bhandar **(Eatery-Snacks)**
Jhalaniyon Ka Raasta **(Wood Carving)**
Khajane Walon Ka Raasta **(Marble
Sculptures)**

Modikhana Chowkdi (ZOOM B)
Sango ka Raasta
Maniharo Ka Raasta
Lal ji Sand ka Raasta **(Lakh Bangles)**
Katta House
Govardhan das ji Havelli
Kala Bhawan
Shri Digamber Jain Mandir Khinducan
Khinduka House
Bajh House
Pandit Shivdeen Haveli
Pandit Shivdeen Ji Ka Raasta **(Copper Works)**
Thathero ka Raasta **(Utensils)**

Chaura Raasta (ZOOM B)
Chaura Raasta **(Gold Minakari)**
Shri Dwarkadheesh Mandir
Tadkeshwar Temple
Mandir Binodi Lal ji
Jaipuri College

Viveshwarji Chowkdi (ZOOM B)
Rana House
Haveli
Gopal ji ka Raasta
Gopal Ji Ka Mandir
Purohit Ji Ka Katla Bazaar **(Sarees)**

Ghat Darwaza Chowkri
Ramganj Bazaar
Haldion Ka Raasta **(Sarees)**
Kanota Haveli
Guddha Thakur Haveli
Banthia Bhawan

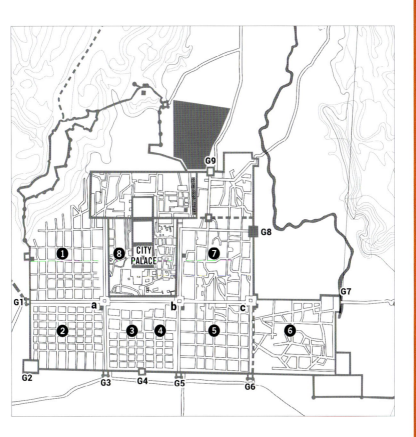

District	Major Nodes	Gates
1. Chowkdi Purani Basti	a. Chhoti Chaupad	G1. Chand Pol
2. Chowkdi Topkhana Desh	b. Badi Chaupad	G2. Singh Dwar
3. Chowkdi Modikhana	c. Ramganj Chaupad	G3. Kishan Pol / Ajmeri Gate
4. Chowkdi Visheshraji		G4. New Gate
5. Ghat Darwaza		G5. Shiv Pol / Sanganeri Gate
6. Chowkdi Topkhana Hazuri		G6. Ghat Gate
7. Chowkdi Ramchandraji		G7. Suraj Pol
8. Chowkdi Sarhad		G8. Char Darwaza
		G9. Dhruv Pol / Jorawar Singh Gate

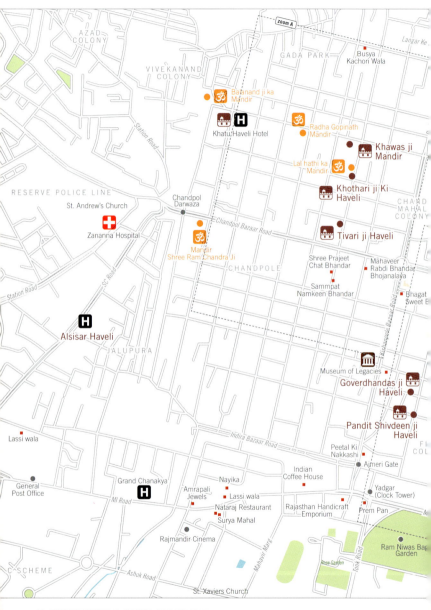

AZAD COLONY

VIVEKANAND COLONY

Station Road

GADA PARK

Langar Ke

zoom A

Busya Kachori Wala

Balanand ji ka Mandir

Khatu Haveli Hotel

Radha Gopinath Mandir

Lal hathi ka Mandir

Khawas ji Mandir

Khothari ji Ki Haveli

CHAND MAHAL COLONY

RESERVE POLICE LINE

St. Andrew's Church

Chandpol Darwaza

Chandpol Bazaar Road

Tivari ji Haveli

Zananna Hospital

Mandir Shree Ram Chandra Ji

CHANDPOLE

Shree Prajeet Chat Bhandar

Mahaveer Rabdi Bhandar Bhojanalaya

Station Road

SC Road

Sammpat Namkeen Bhandar

Bhagat Sweet B

Alsisar Haveli

JALUPURA

Museum of Legacies

Goverdhandas ji Haveli

Pandit Shivdeen ji Haveli

Indira Bazaar Road

Peetal Ki Nakkashi

F COL

Lassi wala

Ajmeri Gate

General Post Office

Grand Chanakya

MI Road

Nayika

Amrapali Jewels

Lassi wala

Nataraj Restaurant

Surya Mahal

Indian Coffee House

Rajasthan Handicraft Emporium

Yadgar (Clock Tower)

Prem Pan

Rajmandir Cinema

C SCHEME

Ashok Road

Mahavir Marg

Rosa Garden

Tonk Road

Ram Niwas Bag Garden

St. Xaviers Church

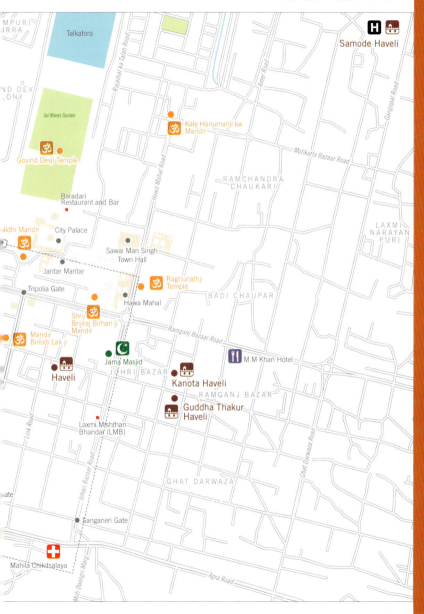

0m 50m 200m ↑ N

MPURI
JRRA

Talkatora

Rajamal ka Talab Road

ND DEV
LONY

Jai Niwas Garden

Kale Hanumanji ka Mandir

Govind Devji Temple

Amer Road

Gangoraj Road

Motikatla Bazaar Road

RAMCHANDRA
CHAUKARI

Baradari
Restaurant and Bar

Hawa Mahal Road

LAXMI
NARAYAN
PURI

Nidhi Mandir   City Palace

Sawai Man Singh
Town Hall

Jantar Mantar

Raghunathji
Temple

Tripolia Gate

BADI CHAUPAR

Hawa Mahal

Shri
Brijiraj Birhari ji
Mandir

Ramganj Bazaar Road

Mandir
Binodi Lak ji

M.M Khan Hotel

Jama Masjid

JOHRI BAZAR

Link Road

Haveli

Kanota Haveli

RAMGANJ BAZAR

Guddha Thakur
Haveli

Laxmi Mishthan
Bhandar (LMB)

Ghat Darwaza Road

GHAT DARWAZA

Johari Bazaar Road

ate

Sanganeri Gate

Mahila Chikitsalaya

Moti Doongri Marg

Agra Road

Chaura Raasta

PRACTICAL INFORMATION:

All major monuments are open to the public, see 'Monuments Timings' p. 210, for details.

Most of the city temples are open to the public from early morning till evening. Unfortunately most of the havelis and private propieties are not open to the public, but no harm asking.

DRONAH Foundation Heritage Walks: 'Chowkri Modikhana' a walk around the Living Culture of Jaipur
www.dronahfoundation.org/heritage-walk/

Jaipur's founder-king Sawai Jai Singh, and many subsequent rulers, understood the importance of city's economic base and therefore promoted a powerful mix of trade and manufacturing activities aimed at Jaipur's long-term prosperity. Foreseeing what city planners today recognize as 'urban economic development,' Jaipur kings paid particular attention to inviting and attracting different kinds of businesses and artisans from India's diverse regions spe-

cializing in particular crafts to their brand-new city. In terms of city's spatial organization, this process, however, entailed two specific phenomena. The first was state support for creating specialized markets, localities, and even entire neighborhoods devoted to a specific economic activity or craft. Stone carving, blue pottery, handmade paper, gold and silver jewelry, gem stone polishing, brass utensils, wood carving and more.

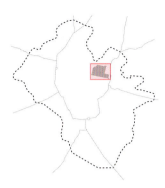

Lac bangles and colored turbans at Sireh Deori Bazaar's shops

The second pillar of the adopted strategy involved inviting and housing entrepreneurs, manufacturers, and craftsmen. The Mughals had promoted a vast range of arts and crafts under their rule and this legacy meant that Jaipur kings could potentially attract entire trades and occupational communities if the terms were attractive. Thus, Jaipur kings offered free land ensuring work-live proximity in earmarked areas that ultimately became famous for particular activities. Agglomeration effects gradually created a rich mix of residential-cum-commercial areas across the entire walled city. So, apart from a diverse range of specialized markets, this itinerary also comprises many *Havelis*, or large courtyard-based houses, that constitute Jaipur's residential fabric and are typically located within walking distance from the bazaars. While touring, pay attention to to the incredible diversity of mixed land-uses that have developed over time.

Purani Basti Chowkdi

Gangauri Bazaar
Nahargarh Rd **(Wooden Hand Blocks)**
Tivari ji Haveli
Lal Hathi ka Mandir
Khothari ji ki Haveli
Purani Basti Raasta
Khawas ji Mandir
Radha Gopinath Mandir
Khatu Haveli Hotel
Balanand ji ka Mandir
Shree Ram Chandra Ji
Chandpol Bazaar

Chandpol Bazar & Topkhana Desh Chowkdi

Chandpol Bazaar
Mahaveer Rabdi Bhandar Bhojanalaya **(Eatery-Sweets)**
Shree Prajeet Chat Bhandar **(Eatery-Sweets)**
Sammpat Namkeen Bhandar **(Eatery-Sweets)**
Jhalaniyon Ka Raasta **(Wood Carving)**
Khajane Walon Ka Raasta **(Marble Sculptures)**

ZOOM A (Purani Basti Chowkdi, Chandpol Baazar and Topkhana Desh Chowkdi)

zoom A

Langar Ke Balaji Ka Rasta

GADA PARK

Nahargrah Road

WOODEN HANDBLOCKS

← Balanand ji ka Mandir

Purani Basti Ka Rasta

Khatu Haveli

Radha Gopinath Mandir

Khawas ji Mandir

Khothari Ji Ki Haveli

Lal Hathi Ka Mandir

Brahmanpuri Road

CHAND MAHAL COLONY

Tivari Ji Haveli

Chandpol Bazaar Road

Shree Prajeet Chat Bhandar

Mahaveer Rabdi Bhandar Bhojanalaya

CHANDPOLE

MARBLE CARVING

Khajane Walon Ka Rasta

Jhalaniyon Ka Rasta

Sammpat Namkeen Bhandar

WOOD CARVING

Kalyan Ji Ka Rasta

Sonkhiyo Ka Rasta

Purani Basti Chowkdi ZOOM A

HAVELIS AND TEMPLES (MANDIR)

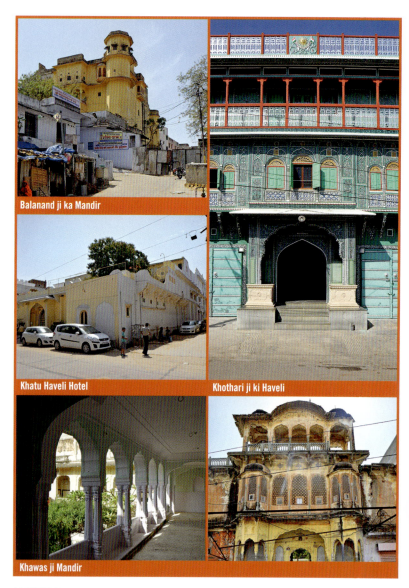

Balanand ji ka Mandir

Khatu Haveli Hotel

Khothari ji ki Haveli

Khawas ji Mandir

Lal Hathi ka Mandir

Tivari ji Haveli

Radha Gopinath Mandir

BAZAARS AND STREET FOOD

Chhoti Chaupad and Flowers Market

Gangauri Bazaar

Chandpol Bazaar and Topkhana Desh Chowkdi

BAZAARS, STREETS (RAASTA), ARTS AND CRAFTS

Chandpol Bazaar

Khajane Walon Ka Raasta

Chandpol Bazaar South Side Elevation

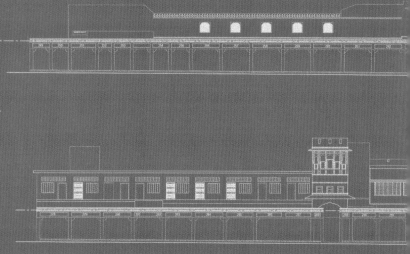

Mishra Raja ji ka Raasta

Baba Harishchandra Marg

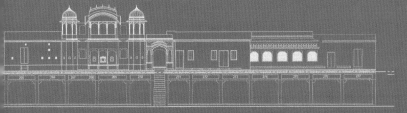

Mishra Raja ji ka Raasta

Baba Harishchandra Marg

Khejro ka Raasta

Modikhana Chowkdi

HAVELIS
Sango ka Raasta
Maniharo Ka Raasta (**Lakh Bangles**)
Lal ji Sand ka Raasta
Katta House
Govardhan das ji Havelli
Kala Bhawan
Shri Digamber Jain Mandir Khinducan
Khinduka House
Bajh House
Pandit Shivdeen Haveli
Pandit Shivdeen Ji Ka Raasta (**Cooper Works**)
Thathero ka Raasta (**Utensils**)

Viveshwarji Chowkdi

Rana House
Haveli
Gopal ji ka Raasta
Gopal Ji Ka Mandir
Purohit Ji Ka Katla Bazaar (**Sarees**)

Ghat Darwaza Chowkdi

Ramganj Bazaar
Haldion Ka Raasta (**Sarees**)
Kanota Haveli
Guddha Thakur Haveli

Chaura Raasta

Chaura Raasta (**Gold Minakari**)
Shri Dwarkadheesh Mandir
Tadkeshwar Temple
Mandir Binodi Lal ji
Jaipuri College

Brij Nidhi Mandir

Jantar Mantar

Raghunathji Temple

Hawa Mahal

Shri Brijiraj Birhari ji Mandir

Sargasuli (Isarlat)

Tripolia Gate

Purohit Ji Ka Katla

Manihara Ka Rasta

Shri Dwarkadhish Mandir

Govt. Public Library

Tadkeshwar Temple

Jama Masjid

JOHRI BAZAR

Mandir Binodi Lak ji

Katta House

Rana House

Gemstone

Gold Jewellery

Girl's College

Gopal Ji/Ka Mandir

Samrat Caterers & Fast Food Restaurant

Haveli 4

Banthia Bhawan

Ishwar Ji Gajak Wale

Kala Bhawan

Chaura Rasta

Gold Minakari

Laxmi Mishthan Bhandar (LMB)

Khinduka House

Goverdhandas ji Havelli

Bajh House

Link Road

Johari Bazar Road

Pandit Shivdeen ji Havelli

Thathero ka Rasta

FILM COLONY

Sahu Restaurant

New Gate

Sanganeri Gate

Indian Ice Cream & Kulfi Faluda

Yadgar (Clock Tower)

MI Road

Mahila Chikitsalaya

HAVELIS

Bajh House

Govardhan das ji Haveli

Kala House

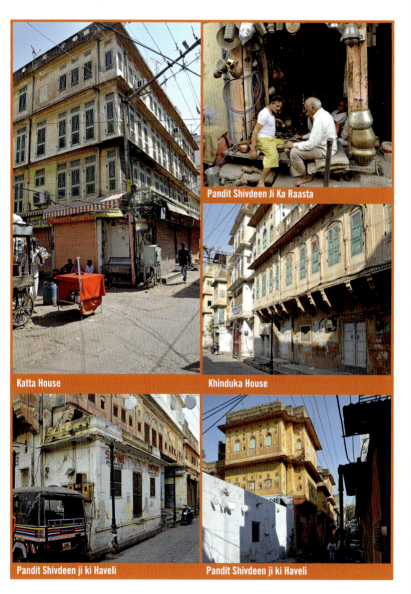

Pandit Shivdeen Ji Ka Raasta

Katta House

Khinduka House

Pandit Shivdeen ji ki Haveli

Pandit Shivdeen ji ki Haveli

Chaura Raasta

HAVELIS, BAZAARS AND TEMPLES (MANDIR)

Mandir Binodi Lal ji Mandir

Tadkeshwar Temple

Chaura Raasta

Viveshwarji Chowkdi

HAVELIS AND TEMPLES (MANDIR)

Haveli

Rana House

Gopal Ji Ka Mandir

Viveshwarji Chowkdi

BAZAARS & STREETS (RAASTA)

Gopal Ji ka Raasta

Purohit Ji Ka Katla Bazaar

Ghat Darwaza Chowkdi

HAVELIS & TEMPLES (MANDIR)

Guddha Thakur Haveli

Kanota Haveli

Haldion Ka Raasta

Starting Point
Sisodiya Rani Garden
1. Ghat ki Guni
2. Sisodiya Rani ka Bagh
3. Vidhyadhar ka Bagh
4. Galta ji
5. Maharaniyon ki Chhatriyan
6. Jal Mahal
7. Kanak Vrindavan
8. Jaigarh Fort
9. Heritage Water Walks (Jaigarh and Nahargarh forts)
10. Nahargarh Fort
11. Gatore ki Chhatriyan
12. Tal Katora

Additional buildings:

A. Lebua Resort

Restaurants:

Once Upon a Time, Madhvendra Palace, Nahargarh Fort
www.onceuponatime.ooo

Toran at Lebua Resort, Jamdoli, Agra Road, Tehsil Ballupura
www.lebua.com

Suria Mahal and Raj Mahal at The Oberoi Rajvillas, Goner Road, Jagdish Colony
www.oberoihotels.com

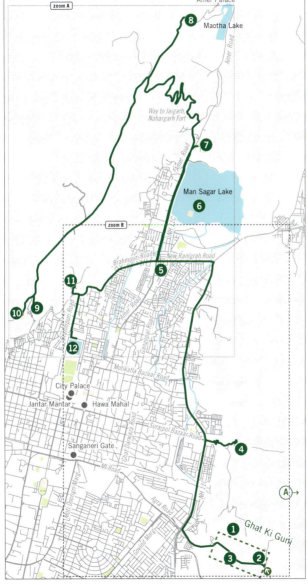

Jaigarh Fort

Maotha Lake

Way to Jaigarh,
Nahargarh Fort

Kanak
Vrindavan

Man Sagar Lake

Petrol Pump

Jal Mahal

New Ramgrah Road

Gaitore Ki
Chhatriyan

Maharaniyon
Ki Chhatriyan

SHANKAR
NAGAR

BADANPURA

Bawadi of
Nahargarh

GANESH
COLONY

Nahargarh
Fort

RAJHANS
COLONY

JOSHI
COLONY

BERAVA
BASTI

BILO DIYAN
MOHALLA

Talkatora

0m   100m   500m

↑ N

zoom B

Gaitore Ki Chhatriyan
⑪

⑤ **Maharaniyon Ki Chhatriyan**

New Ramgrah Road

NH 11C

Amer Road

Brahmpuri Road

SHANKAR NAGAR

BADANPURA

GANESH COLONY

Ajmer Road

Gangwal Road

BILO DIYAN MOHALLA

JOSHI COLONY

Brahmpuri Road

⑫ **Talkatora**

Jai Niwas Garden

Motikatla Bazaar Road

IDGAH KACHI BASTI

RAMCHANDRA CHAUKARI

LAXMI NARAYAN PURI

● City Palace
● Jantar Mantar

● Hawa Mahal

JOHRI BAZAR

RAMGANJ BAZAR

Surajpol Bazaar Road

SURAJPOL

Ghat Darwaza Road

TOPKHANA HAZURI

④ **Galtaji Dham** 🕉

● Sanganeri Gate

MI Road

AUTOMOBILE NAGAR

Moti Doongri Marg

CENTRAL JAIL

BARDIA COLONY

Agra Road

TRANSPORT NAGAR

AMAGAR

NH 11C

Ⓐ →
Lebua Resort

Ⓗ

JANATA COLONY

JADHO KA BAUGH

Mukti Marg

① Ghat Ki Guni

TANEJA BLOCK

Govind Marg

Sisodiya Rani Garden

GURUNANK PURI

②

③

Vidhyadhar Ka Bagh

⓪

Govind Marg

Bhagat Singh Park

Ghat ki Guni

ITINERARY IV **JAIPUR'S REGIONAL LANDSCAPES**

ITINERARY LEVEL: Medium (by car)
DURATION: more than one day
DISTANCE: around 21 km

PRACTCAL INFORMATION:

All major monuments are open to the
public. See 'Monuments Timings' p. 210,
for details.

Most of the temples are open to the public
from early morning till evening.

Ghat ki Kuni Heritage Walk:
www.dronahfoundation.org/heritage-walk/

Heritage Water Walks
Nahargarh Fort:
www.heritagewaterwalks.com/nahargarh-
water-walk/

Jaigarh Fort:
Contact Jaigarh Public Charitable Trust,
City Palace, Jaipur
director@msmsmuseum.com

The hereditary *Maharajas* of Jaipur were sovereign rulers of their territories. Although subservient to the Mughal empire and then the British colonists, often via friendly alliances and formal treaties, they exercised almost unbridled authority within their state. Land was typically perceived as the kingdom's foremost productive asset and, therefore, the royal court paid attention to the entire gamut of land planning and landscape management including the siting of human settlements, building of public works, and the conservation of local ecology. The primary motive was of course economic; because *Lagaan*, or various forms of taxes on the peasants, generated much of state income. Other motives included political control, recreational needs, religious imperatives and the conservation of natural resources for the kingdom's long-term sustainability.

In the Jaipur state, for example, even if all the land ultimately belonged to *Darbar* or

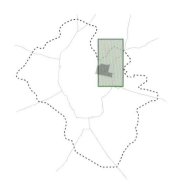

Sisodiya Rani Garden main entrance

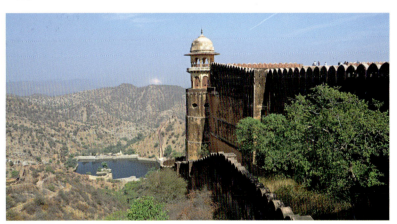

Aerial view from Jaigarh Fort

the King himself, land revenue officials kept detailed records aiming to maintain land's productive usages and wielding the state's authority on the actual ground. In line with the royal preference for hunting and outdoor living, these officials also maintained a sharp gaze upon the territorial landscape looking after critical natural elements like water bodies and open lands. Officials' intimate knowledge of the overall regional landscape and geographical features like natural slopes and watersheds, helped the rulers identify suitable locations for building a diverse range of developmental works, security infrastructure, and civic amenities such as the many military forts, dams, and recreational gardens all around the Jaipur city. This itinerary takes the visitor around some of the more important developments illustrating the purposefully conceived landscape planning and management implemented at the regional scale.

1. Ghat ki Guni

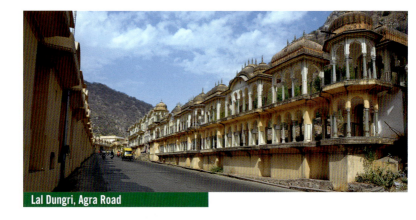

Lal Dungri, Agra Road

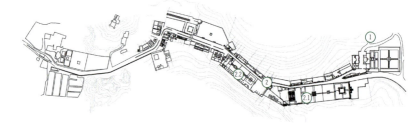

1.   Sisodia Rani ka Bagh
2.   Vidhyadhar ka Bagh entrance
2.1 Roopniwas Bagh
2.2 Vidyadhar ka Bagh

Princely Jaipur was located on a major historical route connecting the nearby city of Ajmer to the Mughal city of Agra. The Mughal nobility routinely undertook pilgrimage to the Ajmer-based Dargah, or shrine, of the famous Sufi saint Khwaja Moinuddin Chisti traveling in sizable caravans via Jaipur. When approaching Jaipur from Agra, the route turns scenic while traversing through a narrow valley situated among steep hills that surround Jaipur's eastern

edge. Ghat ki Guni is a neighborhood-scale ribbon development comprising a continuous band of terrace gardens, temples and havelis straddling both sides of the cleverly engineered thoroughfare sited along this narrow valley.

The purpose is clearly twofold. First, to offer the visitors an impressive prelude of city's prosperity and magnificent spatial form, just before they actually reach Jaipur. The second centered around develop-

Roopniwas Bagh. Agra Road towards Jaipur, Vidhyadhar Ka Bagh at right side

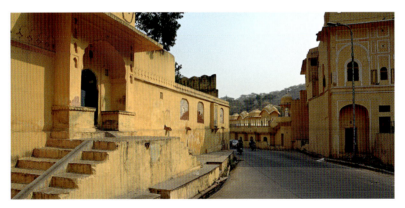

Agra Road, Digamber Jain Mandir main gate at left side

ing a larger hedonistic landscape catering to the ruling elites. In this sense, Ghat Ki Guni, along with many other places in this itinerary, forms part of the extensive recreational landscape that the ruling elites created across scenic settings on the city's edges and proximate areas. This phenomenon exemplifies the thesis that the ruling elites prioritized the many acts of pleasure and recreation over other activities. Wars were not fought frequently and hunting (or *shikar*) was not an everyday pursuit. Captive gardens, leisure locales and getaway properties situated in beautiful and secluded locations provided diverse opportunities for quiet reflection, meditation, music, fellowship and intimate conversations. However, you'll notice, many parts of Ghat ki Guni are not in good condition, demonstrating the strenuous transition from authoritarian royal patronage to India's deepening democracy.

2. Sisodiya Rani ka Bagh Maharaja Sawai Jai Singh - 1728

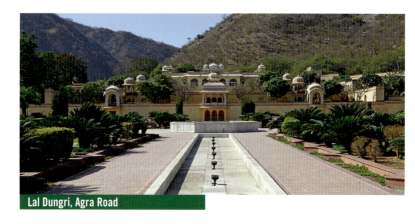

Lal Dungri, Agra Road

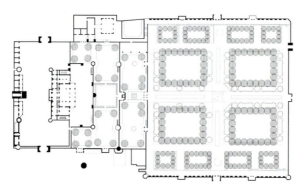

Plan (Palace and Garden)

Jaipur kings, like their counterparts elsewhere, customarily maintained a large contingent of women comprising several wives, close companions and intimate consorts, who they often lavished with gifts and grants. *Sisodiya Rani ka Bagh* literally translates as 'garden of the Sisodiya queen.' It was built by Sawai Jai Singh II in the 18th century, that is almost around the same time as Jaipur's founding, conceivably as a present to a favored queen, who belonged to the Sisodiya clan of Rajputs customarily residing in the Udaipur region. Built using stone and brick masonry covered with lime plaster, the construction methodology is typical for princely Jaipur. As clearly evident in the spatial form, the primary function of Sisodiya Rani ka Bagh is personal pleasure and captive recreation. Exploiting the undulating terrain, the three-tiered garden combines elements of Mughal landscapes like the *Char Bagh* pattern,

Sisodiya Rani ka Bagh

Sisodiya Rani Garden

fountains, water channels and geometrically symmetrical areas. The upper most level of the garden comprises an intimate two-storied palace, with a large hall and beautiful rooms providing just sufficient enclosed space for the royal entourage on a daytrip. Apart from shrines dedicated to Bhagwan Shiva, Vishnu and Hanuman, the campus also houses a variety of semi-covered and open-to-air seating areas that the user could choose depending upon the weather and motive at hand.

Among the few well-preserved places in the entire Ghat Ki Guni, the Sisodiya Rani ka Bagh owes its upkeep to the Public Works Department (PWD). The state agency has done a fair job of conserving this place, even if the many wall paintings and frescos do not match the princely parameters. Once counted among city's preferred marriage and party venues, the Sisodiya Rani ka Bagh has served as a setting for several popular Bollywood movies.

3. Vidhyadhar ka Bagh - Maharaja Sawai Jai Singh (renovation 1988)

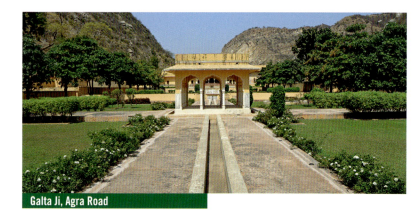

Galta Ji, Agra Road

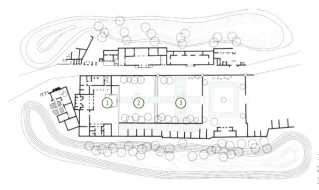

1. Raj Niwas Bagh
2. Vidhyadhar ka Garden
3. Roopniwas Bagh

Vidhyadhar ka Bagh site plan

Vidhyadhar ka Bagh or Vidhyadhar's garden is certainly not as grand as the Sisodiya Rani ka Bagh but definitely important because it celebrates the memory of Vidhyadhar—the architect closely involved in designing Jaipur's plan with the founder king. Per the legend, he belonged to a Brahmin priestly family that had moved to Jaipur from the faraway eastern province of Bengal accompanying the deity of Shila Devi, which Sawai Man Singh carried after his governorship of the area in early 1600s and housed at a temple in the Amer Palace. In the Hindu tradition, the fields of education and religion along with various domains of knowledge are closely identified with Brahmins, who are customarily seen as the custodians of holy texts traditionally written in Sanskrit. Barring a few other occupational groups, a majority of Indians neither needed to study nor had access to formal schooling well until the 20th century. Thus, not surprisingly,

Raj Niwas Bagh, Agra Road

Vidhyadhar ka Garden (also called Roopniwas)

many scholars of Jaipur, finding common grounds between Vidyadhar's Brahmin origins and founder-king Sawai Jai Singh's interest in Sanskrit literature, have asserted that ancient scriptures informed the planning of Jaipur. Pursued more vigorously in recent times, this line of argument advances the thesis that not only the city plan but also its proportions, orientation, and the layout of major buildings are based on the treatises on *Vaastu Vidya,* or the traditional knowledges about city-building and architecture. Notwithstanding the intellectual merit of this debate, it is clear that Vidhyadhar played a pivotal role in composing the city's founding plan under the patronage of a progressive king who, just like any other diligent client, supported his meaningful efforts. When seen from this perspective, Vidhyadhar ka Bagh memorializes an important person who shaped Jaipur's architectural trajectory in fundamental ways.

4. Galta ji Diwan Rao Kriparam - 18th Cent.

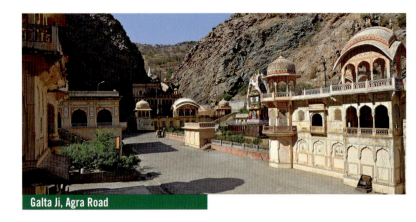

Galta Ji, Agra Road

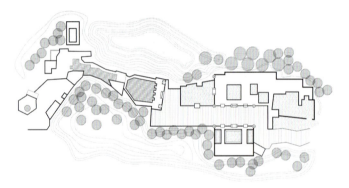

Site plan

Worth visiting for several reasons, Galta ji is primarily a religious place. Originally serving monks and ascetics, this place has now become a popular destination attracting domestic and international tourists. Galta ji comprises a series of elaborate temples and associated buildings built along a narrow opening between sharply rising hills. The slender space purposefully combines open public spaces and water features nes-

tled within ornate architecture creating a pleasing environment.

Legend holds that a famous *Rishi*, or saint, named Galav performed tapasya, or penance, here for a long time. Pleased with the devotion, God blessed him and subsequently a temple was built to mark the event's memory. More recently, however, Diwan Rao Kriparam, a courtier of Sawai Jai Singh II, built the Galtaji Temple in the 18th century, followed by many devotees who

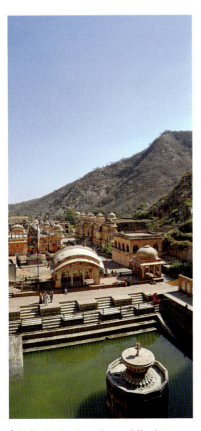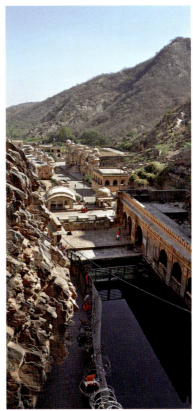

Galta ji natural water springs and *Kunds* (reservoirs)

sponsored other temples and structures. As mentioned before, water is an important religious feature in this part of the world; and here it is rendered even more holy due to the origin from a natural spring. Notice how the builders have designed a series of *Kunds*, or water chambers, that not only capitalize upon the natural flow of spring water but also act as the main structuring element for organizing the physical space. Galta ji is famous for its resident monkeys as well, that many visitors love to feed. Hindu tradition considers many birds and animals holy; associating them with specific gods and deities. The combination of above factors helps Galta ji attract a sizeable congregation around the year including many devotees enjoying a dip in the holy water. Many visitors continue past the highest *kund* reaching a hilltop temple that offers stunning views of the surrounding region.

5. Maharaniyon ki Chhatriyan

Shankar Nagar, Jaipur

The royal ladies cenotaphs, also known as a Maharani ki Chhatri

Women held a significant yet paradoxical position in the princely society. On one hand, they spent their lives sequestered within the bounds of heavily-guarded royal properties, rigid traditional rituals, and elaborate social protocols. On the other, they belonged to the highest possible socio-economic strata; many were literate and independently wealthy; some practiced and patronized creative arts; others routinely sponsored impressive public works like temples and stepwells; or maintained largely autonomous quarters in the zenana and even entire palaces running private households; and frequently participated in the royal court even leading the state as regents, especially when the heir-apparent was a minor. Their power and standing, however, was predicated upon the relationship with the patriarchal guardian. *Maharaniyon ki Chhatriyan* meaning the memorials of the royal ladies marks the funeral spot of many known and unsung women.

6. Jal Mahal Maharaja Sawai Pratap Singh - 1734

Amer Road

Site plan

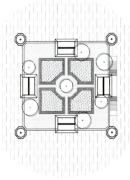

Jal Mahal palace plan

Jal Mahal means water palace. It is located amidst a lake called Man Sagar, which was diligently developed using a natural depression and a strategically-placed dam. Although dilapidated, Jal Mahal is important for several reasons. First, apart from basic human necessity, water was an integral part of both the religious and recreational landscapes in this part of the World. Thus, city-builders always paid careful attention to water planning across spatial scales and you would observe this phenomenon throughout historic Jaipur and the surrounding region. Notice how Jal Mahal, which is essentially a pleasure palace within a water body, merges with the lush greenery of Kanak Vrindavan valley (next stop on this itinerary) that, in turn, becomes part of the hilly landscape surrounding Amer and the adjacent hill forts. Attracting a wide variety of migratory birds, especially in winter months, Jal Mahal remains a popular destination for both city residents and tourists.

7. **Kanak Vrindavan** Maharaja Sawai Jai Singh - 1716

Amer Road, near Jal Mahal

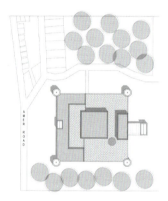

Site plan

The name *Kanak Vrindavan*, *kanak* meaning gold, pays ode to the religiously-famous town of Vrindavan identified closely with Bhagwan Krishna, the playful and adroit incarnation of lord Vishnu. Jaipur's ruling dynasty subscribed to the Vaishnav sect, which prizes devotion to Vishnu above other gods of the Hindu pantheon, and hence the reference to Vrindavan at this place. Located amidst surrounding hills, and toward the end of a lush valley that descends down to Jal Mahal, Kanak Vrindavan is a historic recreational spot that continues to be popular among the general public even today. When seen collectively with other proximate recreational features, the overall regional-scale natural landscape comprising forest preserves, pleasure gardens and pavilions along with water features of various kinds provided diverse opportunities for year-round public recreation and royal pastimes including hunting.

Kanak Vrindavan Gardens

Natwar Ji Ka Mandir, next to the gardens

Kanak Vrindavan's spatial organization and layout comprises all the three main elements that constitute many similarly-planned places in Jaipur and other princely states of Rajasthan, such as Jodhpur, Udaipur, Kota and Bundi, reflecting popular idea about public recreation. The three main elements are: A religious place (usually a temple or locally popular shrine), green open space (usually a park or man-made landscape of trees and foliage), and a water feature (often sited in close proximity). Thus, you'll find that in addition to an elaborate fountain, Kanak Vrindavan has two impressive temples, along with several recreational structures including *Chhatris*, which are open-on-sides pavilions with a dome on the top, facilitating year-round outdoor activities like family get-togethers and picnicking among natural vegetation and flora of different kinds.

8. Jaigarh Fort Maharaja Sawai Jai Singh II - 1726

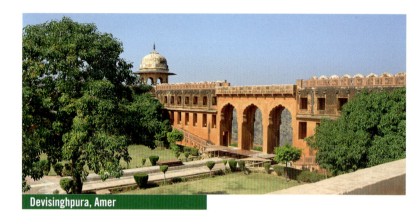

Devisinghpura, Amer

Site plan

Jai means victory and *Garh* means fort. Both Jaigarh and the nearby Nahargarh are military forts, built primarily for royalty's safety and refuge in case of an enemy attack. Thus, not only Jaigarh is linked via (nowadays inaccessible) underground tunnels to the Amer fort but also sited close to Nahargarh for the strategic purposes of quick communication, diversionary attacks, and counterattacks. But Jaigarh serves more of a defense objective than Nahargarh. This comes clear in its design features such as an armory, elaborate rainwater harvesting and storage system, generous provisions for storing basic supplies, and the overall austere nature of its military-oriented architecture that just about provides basic housing and supporting infrastructure such as a garden and a couple temples. Protracted seize of a settlement, allowing nothing in or out, often characterized warfare in this part of the world. Thus, pay attention to builders'

Main fort channel on the right, aproaching the main reservoirs

Water channels and structures

careful designing aimed ultimately at riding out a prolonged seize.

An early ruler of Amer, Kakil Deo laid Jaigarh's foundation in the beginning years of the second millennium after Christ. However, as is true for medieval forts anywhere, it took several generations of dedicated work using mostly involuntary labor, basic tools and sheer human will to complete this massive fort, whose enclosed area measures almost three kilometers in length and a kilometer of width. Refurbished by Sawai Jai Singh, who named it after himself, Jaigarh is perhaps one of the most majestic military forts in India. It also houses a locally famous canon called the *Jaivana*, rumored to be fired only once and never again due to the destruction and aftershocks its produced. Legend holds that Jaipur kings parked their treasure here, but several searches after the end of princely rule yielded nothing.

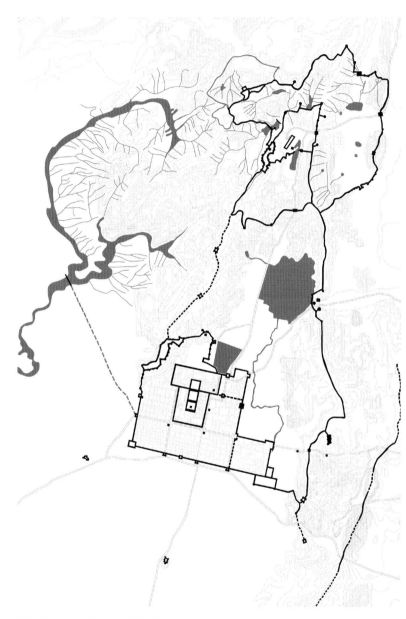

Baori of Nahargarh

Water storage and watershed location at Amber-Jaipur region map (left). Above, Baori of Nahargarh.

Water planning played a key role in fort's overall conceptualization signifying astute design thinking across spatial scales. Apart from basic human needs, water is strategically crucial for riding out a military siege in a hot and dry place. At its heart, however, water planning in these forts pivots around the simple idea of catching every possible raindrop falling in the carefully mapped watershed and then diverting the collected runoff through purposefully designed manmade slopes and gravity-fed channels to a series of storage tanks, locally called *Tankas*. Given the region's history of persistent droughts and distinctive monsoonal climate, characterized by either heavy rains or dry months, the enabling infrastructure is cleverly engineered to cleanse and hold enormous amount of freshwater for a variety of everyday and warfare purposes.

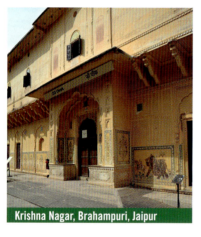

Krishna Nagar, Brahampuri, Jaipur

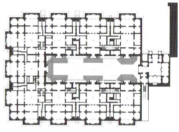

Floor plan

Elevations

Nahar means tiger and *Garh* means fort. So, a literal translation of *Nahargarh* is Tiger-fort. However, a parallel legend posits that Nahargarh derives its name from Nahar Singh who was a *Bhomia*, or guardian angel of this land, that grew unhappy with the prospect of encroachment upon his property but reconciled when the fort was named after him and a temple built in his honor at Nahargarh. Notwithstanding the tales around name's origin, Nahargarh

along with the adjoining and much older Jaigarh, comprises part of the Jaipur's security architecture that the kings began to strengthen after acquiring prosperity in the late 16th century. Sawai Jai Singh, sponsored major works in *Nahargarh*, followed by Sawai Ram Singh and finally, Sawai Madho Singh who patronized the building of Madhvendra Bhawan, a small but elegant palace built mainly for recreational purposes, at the turn of the 19th century.

Fort main facade and top roof (above)

Compared to the militaristic orientation of Jaigarh, Nahargarh, however, is conceived more as a royal retreat offering getaway accommodation and privacy for the king amidst picturesque views of the city and surrounding landscapes including the Man Sagar lake, Jal Mahal palace and Kanak Vrindavan that you just visited. Nahargarh also has a *Diwan-i-Aam,* or the hall of public audience, indicating that the kings were not averse to commoners' access into the fort, unlike Jaigarh where purportedly even the crown-prince was not allowed to enter unless called by the Maharaja himself. Pay attention to the careful efforts building massive infrastructure and supporting amenities for royal comforts in safe and secluded settings. Also notice the remnants of fortification and watchtowers among the sweeping views of the surrounding hilly terrain that facilitated watch and guard across the distant horizon.

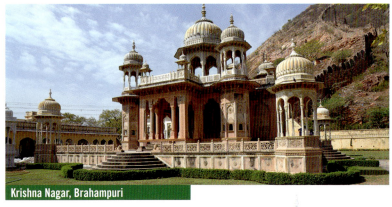

Krishna Nagar, Brahampuri

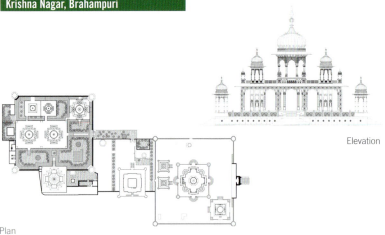

Elevation

Plan

Building cenotaphs, or a memorial to commemorate an important and dear person after their death, was a traditional custom among the ruling families in this region. Thus, apart from Jaipur, you find excellent examples in nearby places like Jodhpur, Jaisalmer and Udaipur. Employing the *chhatri*, literally an umbrella or domed pavilion, as the basic building block, cenotaphs are typically built on the site of cremation. A characteristic feature of Rajput architectural tradition, cenotaphs symbolize the practice of ancestor worship which is, in turn, predicated upon the notion of preserving the memory of a person by providing permanence to their name. Gaitore ki Chhatriyan comprise a group of memorials collectively marking the cremating grounds for the male members of the Jaipur royal family. Good idea to stop en route to / from Amer for visiting some of the more beautiful *chhatris* like that of the founder-king Sawai Jai Singh II.

12. Tal Katora - Maharaja Sawai Jai Singh II

Bhrampuri Road, Tal Katora

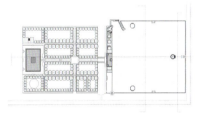

Plan

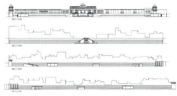

Sections

Tal Katora literally means a pond shaped like a bowl. This manmade reservoir and the adjoining Raja Mal Ka Talab, or Raja Mal's lake, were developed using a natural depression at the time of Jaipur's founding for providing a permanent water feature within the palace complex. Adjoining landscaped areas and pavilions like the Badal Mahal and *Chattris* offered both captivating views and a variety of recreational options for royal pastime. When viewed from the vantage of larger spatial scale, Tal Katora formed part of the broader regional-level water and landscape systems that the Jaipur's rulers and peoples developed all around the proximate Amer area with interlinking mechanisms for water transfer and recharge of the overall water-table. Unfortunately, due to the vagaries of monsoon, apathetic governments and poor upkeep, *Tal Katora* seldom receives adequate water while the Raja Mal lake was leveled and subdivided into plots.

133

A. Lebua Resort Ar. P. Nath and A. Thanawala (Urban Studio) - 2012

Jamdoli, Agra Road, Tehsil Ballupura

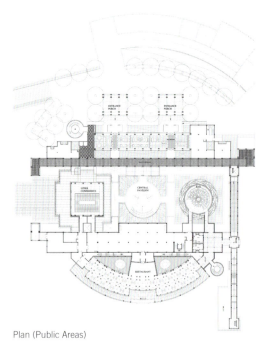

Plan (Public Areas)

Hence Devi Ratan is a hotel that is informed by the culture and aesthetics of traditional Rajasthan but transcends it to form its own contemporaneity and expression in 21th century India.

Hotel's suites details, each room is unique coloured.

Emerald green, Ruby red, orange Coral, yellow Sapphire give the project its unique colour coding

Lebua Resort has been conceptualized as a modern luxury hotel. Formerly known as Devi Ratan, it takes its name from the *Nav Ratn* nine pure gemstones that are said to focus the cosmic energy of an associated celestial body, ruled by a diety.

One of the first and most striking impressions of the hotel is the bold colour scheme. The vibrant *Nav ratna* colours have informed the colour palate at Devi Ratan.

Modern techniques of conception and production have helped to create contemporary patterns. Reminiscent of the past, each pattern combines the aesthetics of the present with the emotional values of the past and forms an eclectic language which has been used through the project ranging from the architectural scale to the interior and product scale of accessories, cutlery and textiles.

Starting Point

0. New Gate
1. Ramniwas Bagh Garden
2. Albert Hall Museum
3. Maharaja College
4. Maharani College
5. Central Park
6. Birla Planetarium and Science Center
7. Statue Circle
8. Secretariat
9. Rajasthan High Court
10. Vidhan Sabha
11. Jaipur Nagar Nigam

Additional buildings:

A. Saint Xavier School & Church
B. Royal Ensign Apartments
C. Reserve Bank of India

Cafes and Restaurants:

Shopping:

Cafe Palladio
100 Jawahar Lal Nehru Marg, Rambagh
www.bar-palladio.com

Fabindia,
B4-E Prithviraj Road, Opposite Central Park
Gate No. 4, C Scheme
www.fabindia.com

Tapri The Tea House
B4-E Prithviraj Road, Opposite Central Park
Gate No. 4, C Scheme
www.tapri.net

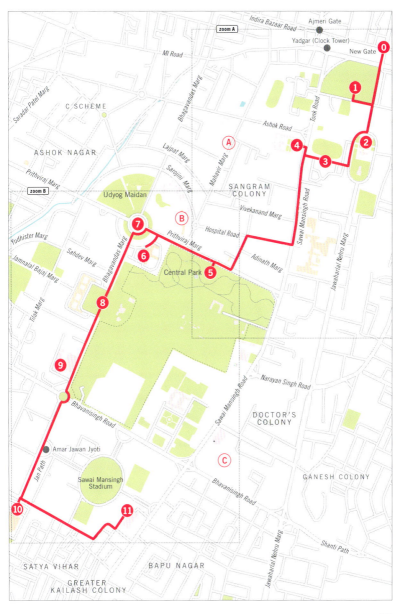

Film Colony

Ajmeri Gate

Indian Coffee House

Nayika   Tholia Building

Yadgar (Clock Tower)

New Gate   **0**

Lassi wala

Rajasthan Handicraft Emporium

Prem Pan

Nataraj Restaurant

MI Road

Panch Batti

Surya Mahal

Ram Niwas Bagh Garden

Rajmandir Cinema

1

Rose Garden

Tonk Road

St. Xaviers Church

Ashok Road

A

Albert Hall Museum   **2**

St. Xaviers School

Maharavi Marg

WC

4

Maharani College

Maharaja College

3

Nehru Garden

Hotel Diggi Palace

H

SANGRAM COLONY

Vivekanand Marg

Sawai Maansingh Road

Jawaharlal Nehru Marg

Hospital Road

Colonial Bungalows

Tapri The Tea House

C-SCHEME

Fabindia

Adinath Marg

Sawai Maansingh Hospital

5

Central Park

Doongri Marg

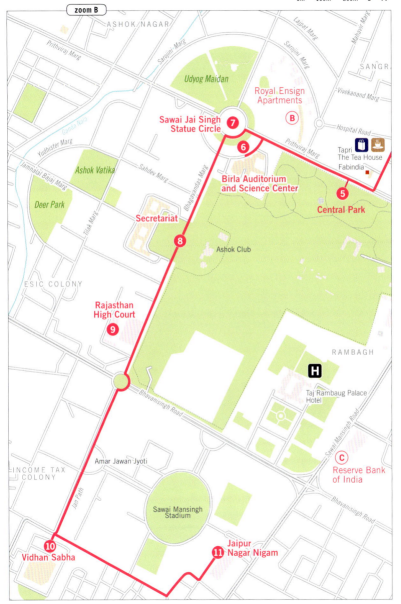

zoom B

ASHOK NAGAR

Prithviraj Marg

Sarojini Marg

Lajpat Marg

Mahavir Marg

Udyog Maidan

Royal Ensign Apartments

SANGR

Vivekanand Marg

Sarojini Marg

Sawai Jai Singh Statue Circle **7**

B

Hospital Road

Prithviraj Marg

6

Genda Nala

Yudhister Marg

Ashok Vatika

Sahdev Marg

Birla Auditorium and Science Center

Tapri The Tea House Fabindia

Jamnalal Bajaj Marg

Deer Park

Bhagwandas Marg

5

Central Park

Tilak Marg

Secretariat

8

Ashok Club

ESIC COLONY

RAMBAGH

Rajasthan High Court

9

H

Taj Rambaug Palace Hotel

Bhavanisingh Road

Sawai Mansingh Road

INCOME TAX COLONY

Amar Jawan Jyoti

C

Reserve Bank of India

Jan Path

Bhavanisingh Road

Sawai Mansingh Stadium

10
Vidhan Sabha

Jaipur Nagar Nigam
11

0m   100m   200m   ↑ N

Chaura Rasta, Nehru Bazar

ITINERARY V **PUBLIC AND CIVIC ARCHITECTURE**

ITINERARY LEVEL: medium (by foot/
autorickshaw/car)
DURATION: one day
DISTANCE: around 5 km

PRACTICAL INFORMATION:

The Albert Hall Museum and major
monuments are open to the public. See
'Monuments Timings' p. 210, for details.

Unfortunately most of the Government
buildings like the Vidhan Sabha
(Parliament) and private institutions are
not open to the public.

This itinerary tracks the development of Jaipur's civic and public architecture built outside the city wall from mid-19th century onwards. The multi-talented Sawai Ram Singh (1852-1880) first patronized 'modern' public works, altering the city's architectural trajectory in fundamental ways. After ruthlessly crushing the great rebellion of 1857, British pressure over native princes to 'modernize' grew steadily. Thus, among other administrative reforms,

Sawai Ram Singh created a Public Works Department (PWD) employing the prolific colonial engineer Swinton Jacob. The PWD introduced new ideas and typologies while commissioning diverse city-improvement projects like municipal lighting, water supply, schools, museum and a hospital. It also advanced the distinctive design approach of eclectically combining building elements from different regional traditions that Jacob laboriously documented in his

The Albert Hall Museum, main facade.

majestic *Jeypore Portfolio of Architectural Details*. But Sawai Ram Singh simultaneously sought to preserve princely autonomy by maintaining a conventional lifestyle and patronizing the parallel institution of *Raj Imaraat* which, overseen by local personnel, undertook Maharaja's personal construction projects that continued to be built in the traditional manner. He also ordered the walled city painted uniformly—rather idiosyncratically to celebrate the Edward VII maiden visit in 1876—earning Jaipur the sobriquet of 'Pink city'. Not surprisingly, PWD buildings stand out in contrast with the walled city, like the Albert Hall museum (by Swinton Jacobs), that are setback from the property line, surrounded by formally landscaped areas, and built with dressed-stone masonry in the 'Indo-Saracenic style' prevalent across British-Indian cities like Mumbai.

1. **Ramniwas Bagh Garden** Maharaja Sawai Ram Singh - 1868

Jawahar Lal Nehru Marg, Ram Niwas Garden

Site plan

Commissioned in 1868, the Ram Niwas Bagh is only-one-of-its-kind of development in Jaipur's architectural history. Conceived as an open-to-public civic campus located just outside the walled city, the overall complex comprises a formally-designed public park, a museum (described next), botanical and zoological gardens, city's first modern hospital, and a public theater that the authorities added latter. The idea here is clearly two-fold: first, to create a di-verse range of cutting-edge civic facilities befitting a progressive princely state; the second, to provide recreational opportunities to general public matching the highest standards anywhere in the British empire. For instance, the large well-maintained gardens and the open public spaces attracted a steady stream of city residents including a regular audience for the impressive Jaipur state military band that turned out per the set calendar.

2. Albert Hall Ar. Sir Samuel Swinton Jacob - 1868

Museum Road, Ram Niwas Garden

Front elevation

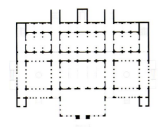

Ground floor and first floor plans

One of the many celebratory events marking the British emperor (Albert) Edward VII visit in 1876 included the ground-breaking of Albert Hall. Originally conceived as a town hall, the impressive structure was repurposed as an open-to-public state museum upon completion. Designed and supervised by Swinton Jacob, with notable support from Jaipur's resident surgeon and art-enthusiast Dr. Thomas Hendley, the floridly decorated structure is one of Jaipur's iconic buildings. The building plan is symmetrically organized comprising a series of differently-sized halls suitable for a variety of displays. The collection itself comprises artifacts collected from India's distinct regions and specimens of local arts and crafts. The building's external form, combining diverse elements from a variety of building traditions, is a prominent example of Indo-Saracenic style that the state PWD introduced into Jaipur's spatial form.

3. Maharaja College Maharaja Sawai Ram Singh II - 1844

Sawai Ram Singh Road

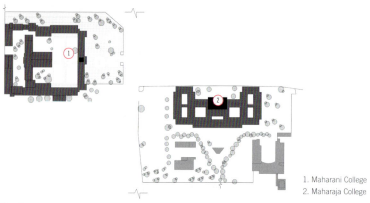

1. Maharani College
2. Maharaja College

Site plan

The chiefs of princely states, were largely averse to introducing modern 'western-style' education in their kingdoms because it could seed critical thinking and political dissent among their subjects. The colonists, on the other hand, began setting up educational facilities from the early-19th century in British Indian cities for the express purpose of training manpower useful in furthering the colonial enterprise. Sawai Ram Singh created Maharaja's school in 1844 for imparting modern education to local boys. The institution grew over time eventually becoming the Maharaja college. Originally affiliated with the University of Calcutta, the Maharaja college finally became a constituent college of the University of Rajasthan founded in 1947. Built in Indo-Saracenic style, the pioneering institution is an important marker in the development of Jaipur's civic architecture aimed at promoting public good.

4. Maharani College Maharani Gayatri Devi - 1944

Sawai Ram Singh Road

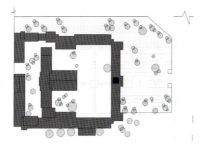

Site plan

Despite the steady development of modern amenities and public facilities in princely Jaipur, the society's overall disposition remained comparatively conservative with the *purdah* system (segregation of sexes) being widespread and the education of girls not very common well until the 20th century. Maharani Gayatri Devi, popularly known by her initials MGD, the princess of Cooch Behar and later the third and youngest wife of Jaipur's last reigning ruler Sawai Man Singh II, pioneered girls' education by promoting the first education centers reserved exclusively for girls (named Maharani college and [the nearby] MGD school in her honor) during the early 1940s. Her autobiography, *A Princess Remembers: The Memoirs of the Maharani of Jaipur,* provides an insightful account of changes in Jaipur during the second half of the 20th century including the resistance that she faced promoting these pioneering institutions.

5 . Central Park

Prithviraj Road, Rambagh

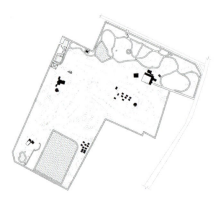

Site plan

One of the few outright successful efforts of Jaipur Development Authority, Central Park quickly gained popularity after opening few years ago. Conceived as a city-level park, this place's history goes back to Jaipur's last ruler Sawai Man Singh II, who promoted outward-oriented development via new neighborhoods like the 'C scheme' that houses Central Park. Trained under the British resident's watchful eye, Sawai Man Singh was thoroughly anglicized. He routinely spent summers in London, famously headed Jaipur's Polo team, and chose to live in the refurbished garden palace of Rambagh, spread over a large city block comprising a polo ground and golf course. After the abolition of princely rule, authorities took over many royal properties and, after long-litigation and turning-down competing proposals for commercial development, created Central Park on part of the Rambagh palace's substantial grounds.

6. Birla Planetarium and Science Center B.M. Birla - 1960s-1980s

Prithviraj Road, Near Statue Circle, Rambagh

Site plan

This campus comprises several buildings including a planetarium, science center and associated facilities like a library and lecture halls, an auditorium, a variety of exhibition spaces and sizable open lawns. Sponsored by the non-profit arm of India's leading business house known by the family name Birla, the overall architecture of this campus fits the institutional genre dominant in the last quarter of the 20th century. Practiced both by public-sector agencies like the PWD and large design firms, this approach is characterized by the generous use of sandstone tiles cladded over reinforced cement concrete (RCC) framed structure, clean geometry of the external form, and token gesture to regional history via faux arches, chattris and other notable architectural elements like the Amer's famous Ganesh Pol, replicated here as the auditorium's main entrance.

7. Statue Circle Maharaja Jai Singh II

C Scheme, Ashok Nagar

Site plan

Located at the heart of affluent neighborhood called 'C Scheme,' Statue Circle also doubles-up as a popular gathering place for city residents. The C Scheme is a bungalow-style garden suburb conceived during the early 1940s under the premiership of Mirza Ismail (1941-44). Before coming to Jaipur, Mirza had served at the princely state of Mysore working closely with the German architect and planner, Otto Koenigsberger, who had introduced him to contemporary city design ideas like planned neighborhoods. Although, Jaipur's first residential extension named *New Colony* had been developed in 1932, Mirza's brief tenure witnessed the rapid development of several new neighborhoods such as C-scheme, promptly patronized by local elites who, preferring modern bungalows over traditional havelis, had already began migrating from the walled city following Maharaja's own example.

8. Secretariat Maharaja Man Singh - late 1930s

Bhagwantdas Road, C Scheme, Janpath

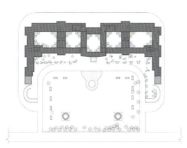

Site plan

The Secretariat campus comprises several buildings that house the centralized bureaucracy of Rajasthan State including all the ministers, secretaries, and other higher officials in one place. Built by the PWD in late Indo-Saracenic style, the Main Building, visible from the Bhagwan Das Road, matches the original purpose of barracks for Sawai Man Guards, an elite unit of the princely army. Like many contemporary kings, Maharaja Man Singh was fond of his state military and actively supported British efforts in the two great wars. The princely army's main base was the Jaipur cantonment (near Hasanpura) while crack detachments entrusted with royal security were stationed at the city place next to Hawa Mahal (called Rajendra Hazari Guards), part of which moved to this location when the Maharaja made Rambagh palace his primary residence. It was repurposed after the abolition of princely rule.

9. Rasjasthan High Court State PWD - 1949

Bhagwantdas Road, C Scheme, Janpath

Built by the state PWD in two phases, this campus houses the Jaipur bench of Rajasthan state's apex court located at the city of Jodhpur. The main building reflects the distinctive design approach, centered upon using dressed-stone masonry and clean geometry of spatial form, which the state PWD gradually developed over time for public and civic buildings as you have seen all along the itinerary.

10. Vidhan Sabha (Parliament of Rajasthan) State PWD - 1994-2001

Pankaj Singhvi Marg, Jyothi Nagar, Lalkothi

Since the founding of Rajasthan state, the legislature continued to meet in the Sawai Man Singh Town Hall. Conceived conventionally using the traditional design palette, this imposing building, in addition to other public buildings along the *Jan Path* or people's street, illustrates the conservative worldview of state architects.

11. Jaipur Nagar Nigam Uttam C. Jain Architects - 1992

Tonk road, Lal Kothi

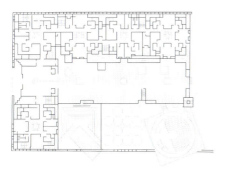

Plan

Jaipur Nagar Nigam translates as Jaipur Municipal Corporation (JMC). The idea of municipal governance goes back to Sawai Ram Singh, who sponsored a municipality in 1868 with 26 nominated members. The institution grew incrementally from a nominated municipal council to a full-fledged democratically-elected municipal corporation in 1994. Around the same time, JMC decided to build a new building, selecting the Bombay-based design firm of Uttam C. Jain. Similar to other first-generation architects of post-independence India, like Charles Correa and B. V. Doshi, Jain's work has centered around the philosophy of conceiving a contemporary architecture for an independent country, while searching for a suitable modern vocabulary that matches the needs and aspirations of its diverse people and the rich building traditions of disparate cultural regions. Notice how the JMC campus derives inspiration from Jaipur's city plan and spatial form.

151

A. Saint Xavier School and Church

Bhagwandas Road, C Scheme

Site plan School

Site plan Church

Saint Xavier School is both part of a national chain and a famous local institution located at the heart of C-Scheme area. Originally conceived as a small-scale boys-only institution in the 1940s, the public school grew when Maharaja Sawai Man Singh II gave this land virtually free to serve the purpose of quality education. Built in the trademark austere design style—using dressed-stone masonry, simple geometric form and no ostentation—routinely employed in church-sponsored institutions, the school buildings and a modest church are sited among generous playgrounds and cutting-edge sporting facilities. Important to note that Christian missionaries have done pioneering work across India in the field of education and healthcare. Saint Xavier institutions are sponsored by Jesuits. Many of Jaipur's notable leaders, government officials, leading professionals and businessmen graduated from this school.

B. Royal Ensign Apartments

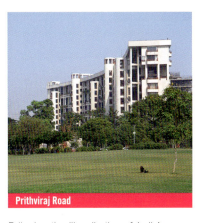

Prithviraj Road

Site plan

Following the liberalization of India's economy beginning early 1990s, the focus of authorities shifted to promoting real-estate development with the help of private sector. Designed by a large-scale multi-disciplinary Delhi-based consulting firm called Planning Design Bureau (PDB) for a private builder, the Royal Ensign apartment project exemplifies the larger turn toward global trends in the country's approach to architecture.

C. Reserve Bank of India Kothari and Associates - 1980s

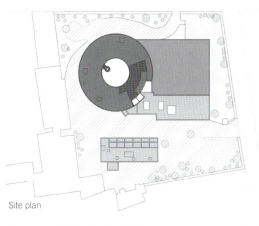

Site plan

Reserve Bank of India (or RBI) is the country's central bank based at Bombay with several regional centers in intermediate cities like Jaipur. Apparently inspired by the shape of a stack of coins and a wad of notes, this structure fits well with other contemporary modernist developments described in itinerary VII covering JLN Marg.

Starting Point

Hotel Diggi Palace

1. Hotel Diggi Palace
2. Grand Uniara
3. Narain Niwas Palace
4. Rambagh Palace
5. Rajmahal Palace
6. Hari Mahal Palace
7. Taj Jai Mahal Palace
8. Alsisar Haveli
9. Shahpura House

Additional buildings:

A. Collectorate Circle Park
B. Mathur's Residence
C. Zanana Hospital
D. Saint Andrews Church
E. All Saints Church
F. General Post Office (GPO)
G. Hotel Khasa Kothi
H. ITC Rajputana

Cafes and Restaurants:

Anokhi Cafe
2nd Floor, KK Square, Prithviraj Road, C Scheme
www.anokhicafe.com

Bar Palladio
Kanota Bagh, Narain Singh Road, Rambagh
www.bar-palladio.com

Home Cafe by Mr.Beans, Sardar Patel Marg, C Scheme

Kanji Sweets & Restaurant, Opposite Polo Victory Cinema, Station Road, Gopalbari

Nibs Cafe & Chocolataria, Bhawani Singh Marg, near MGF Mall, C Scheme
www.nibscafe.com

On The House (OTH), Durgadas Colony, C Scheme

The Forresta, Devrajniwas, near Moti Mahal Cinema, Bani Park

Shopping:

Anantaya
The Kanota, Narain Niwas Palace, Opposite City Pulse Mall, Narayan Singh Rd
www.anantayadecor.com

Anokhi, 2nd Floor, KK Square, Prithviraj Road, C Scheme
www.anokhi.com

Cottons Jaipur, Hari Mahal Palace, Jacob Road, Civil Lines

Crossword Bookstore, First Floor, KK Square, Prithvi Raj Marg, C Scheme
www.crossword.in

Fabindia, Barwara Kothi, 5 First Floor, Jacob road, Civil Lines
www.fabindia.com

Good Earth Jaipur, Rajmahal Palace Hotel, Sardar Patel Marg, C Scheme

Kilol Jaipur, Sardar Patel Marg, C Scheme
www.kilol.com

Suvasa, 5 Jacob Road, Civil Lines
www.suvasa.in

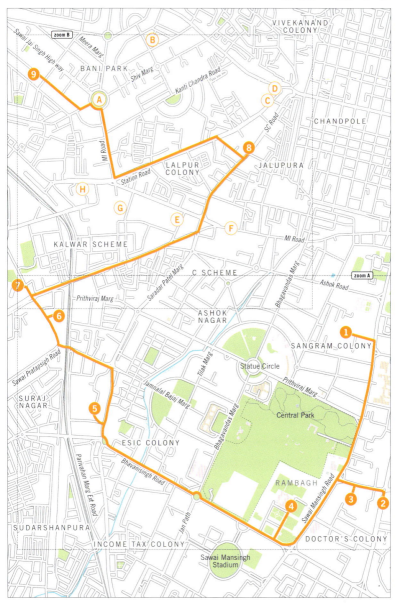

ZOOM A

zoom A

Taj Jai Mahal Palace

7

Jaipur Road

Fabindia
Suvasa

Cottons

Jacob Marg

Prithviraj Marg

6 **Hari Mahal Palace**

Neerja International
Blue Pottery

Chief Ministers Residence

Sawai Pratapsigh Road

Parivahan Marg

Jamnalal Bajaj Marg

Saradar Patel Marg

Anokhi

Crossword
Bookstote

Prithviraj Marg

Azad Marg

Yudhister Marg

Jamnalal Bajaj Marg

Ashok Vat.

Deer Park

Tilak Marg

SURAJ NAGAR

Rajmahal Palace

5

Kilol Jaipur

On The House

Home Cafe
by Mr.Beans

MGF Metropolitan Mall

Bais Godam Flyover

Nibs Cafe

22 Godam
Circle

ESIC COLONY

GEEJGARH VIHAR
COLONY

Nehru
Sahkar Bhavan

Parivahan Marg Ext Road

Bhavanisingh Road

BAIS GODAM

SUDARSHANPURA

SHARMA
COLONY

An

INCOME TAX COLONY

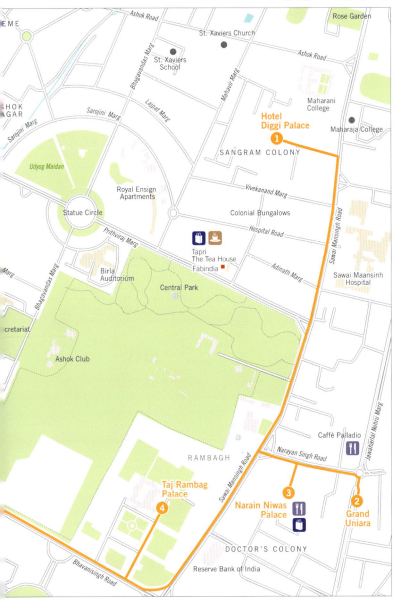

Rose Garden

Ashok Road

St. Xaviers Church

Ashok Road

EME

Bhagavandas Marg

St. Xaviers
School

Mahavir Marg

Maharani
College

Lajpat Marg

HOK
AGAR

Sarojini Marg

Sarojini Marg

**Hotel
Diggi Palace**

1

Maharaja College

SANGRAM COLONY

Udyog Maidan

Royal Ensign
Apartments

Vivekanand Marg

Sawai Mansingh Road

Statue Circle

Colonial Bungalows

Prithviraj Marg

Hospital Road

Tapri
The Tea House
Fabindia

Birla
Auditorium

Adinath Marg

Sawai Maansinh
Hospital

Marg

Bhagvandas Marg

Central Park

cretariat

Ashok Club

Caffé Palladio

Jawaharlal Nehru Marg

Narayan Singh Road

R A M B A G H

Sawai Mansingh Road

**Taj Rambag
Palace**

3

2

4

**Narain Niwas
Palace**

**Grand
Uniara**

DOCTOR'S COLONY

Bhavanisingh Road

Reserve Bank of India

ZOOM B

zoom B

Sawai Jai Singh High way

Jas Vilas **H**

Meera Marg

B Mathur's Residence

BANI PARK

Meera Marg

Shiv

H

H

9
Shahpura House

Umaid Mahal

Umaid Bhawan
Hotel

BANI PARK

Kanti Chand

H

Traditional
Heritage Haveli

Shiv Marg

D Circle Park

A
Collectorate
Circle Park

Kabir Marg

Kanti Chandra Road

MI Road

Kanji Sweets &
Restaurant **🍴**

LALP
COLO

🍴 The Forresta

H **H**
ITC Rajputana

Station Road

H **i**
Hotel Khasa Kothi **G**

Sanjay Marg

🍴
Bhagat
Mithai Bhandar

All Saints Church **E**

KALWAR SCHEME

Taj Jai Mahal Palace

7

Jaipur Road

Prithviraj Marg

Sardar Patel Marg

Fabindia
Suvasa

Cottons

Alsisar Haveli
www.alsisarhaveli.com

Arya Niwas
www.aryaniwas.com

Grand Uniara
www.granduniara.com

Harimahal Palace Hotel
www.harimahalpalace.com

Hotel Diggi Palace
www.hoteldiggipalace.com

Hotel Khasa Kothi
www.rtdc.in

ITC Rajputana
www.itchotels.in

Jas Vilas
www.jasvilas.com

Leisure inn Grand Chanakya
www.leisureinngrandchanakya.in

Narain Niwas Palace
www.hotelnarainniwas.com

Rambagh Palace
www.taj.tajhotels.com

Rajmahal Palace Hotel
www.rajmahalpalacejaipur.com

Shahpura House
www.shahpura.com

Taj Jai Mahal Palace
www.taj.tajhotels.com

Umaid Bhawan
www.umaidbhawan.com

Umaid Mahal
www.umaidmahal.com

Diggi House, Shivaji Marg, C Scheme

ITINERARY LEVEL: Medium (by car)
DURATION: More than one day
DISTANCE: around 10 km

PRACTICAL INFORMATION:

Rajasthan Directorate of Tourism,
Paryatan Bhawan, Khasa Kothi Hotel
Campus, M.I.Road
www.tourism.rajasthan.gov.in

Due to the inherent space constraints of
a travel guide, our city hotels coverage
cannot be exhaustive at all. See "Facts for
the Visitor," p. 198, for additional details.

Reflecting the importance of tourism for Jaipur's economic base, the city hosts a wide variety of differently-designed hotels. This itinerary provides a brief tour covering some of the more notable places, varying substantially in history, layout and design. Unfortunately, due to the inherent space constraints of a travel guide, our coverage cannot be exhaustive at all.

The representative examples described below cover two main kind of development approaches. Purpose-built hotels represent deliberate design efforts at the time of their conception. The other kind involves repurposing existing properties into a 'heritage hotel,' locally-popular term denoting an old haveli, mansion, or palace converted into a boutique hotel. Supervised carefully by their owners, typically still-in-residence, each place is unique in character, illustrating long-term evolution of historic buildings shaped by successive generations of fam-

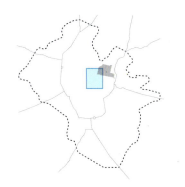

Interiors of Harimahal Palace, showcasing some of the Royal Family memories

ily-owners in line with the changing conditions and preferences over time.

Many royal palaces, as well as the minor nobility's relatively-moderate havelies and mansions, were originally conceived as secondary residences. Maharajas typically maintained several palaces in addition to the main city palace while many Rajas and Thakurs, or largely autonomous rulers of ancestral estates, in addition to the family-seat or principal residence at their native place, customarily maintained a townhouse at Jaipur. Typically surrounded by large grounds and orchards, many of these places ringed around the city walls; collectively creating both a circle of protection and series of green landscapes on the urban periphery. Even as the surrounding lands have been subdivided and sold in recent times, the tourism boom has rejuvenated these distinct examples of Jaipur's princely patrimony.

1. Hotel Diggi Palace (www.hoteldiggipalace.com)

Diggi House, Shivaji Marg, C Scheme

The large Diggi House, rechristened as Diggi Palace after repurposing into a hotel during the 1980s, is spread over 18 acres. Sited at a prominent location along the arterial road leading to Ajmeri Gate, the property's incremental development beginning in the 1860s coincided with Sawai Ram Singh led creation of civic infrastructure in this area (see itinerary V). Location of a nobility's Jaipur house typically indicated their relation and proximity to the princely court. One of Jaipur Maharaja's brother had inherited the proximate villages and the settlement of Diggi, famous for an annual religious fair centered upon a temple dedicated to Bhagwan Krishna. Comprising several buildings, open spaces and gardens, the Diggi palace complex showcases an eclectic mix of architectural elements that the successive owners experimented with. Large grounds make it possible to host the now-famous Jaipur Literature Festival and several other expos year-around.

The *Darbar* hall or large congregation space that traditionally hosted royal gatherings and functions

Courtyard Haveli suites on left, and The Baradari Mahal Restaurant

2. Grand Uniara (www.granduniara.com)

Jawaharlal Nehru Marg, Near Trimurti Circle

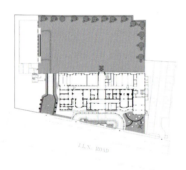

Site plan

East and west elevations

Grand Uniara is one of the city's newest heritage hotel opened a few years ago. Located about 140 kilometers southeast of Jaipur, the principality of Uniara maintained a certain level of independence from Jaipur state; the kings of Uniara were closely related to Jaipur's ruling family and carried the honorific title of *Rao Rajas*. This particular property comprised large grounds (or Bagh) surrounding a relatively-modest mansion built around the turn of the 19th century. The Bagh was subdivided and sold (although still known as Uniara Bagh 'colony,' an Indian euphemism for a neighborhood) in the 1970s following the imposition of 'land-ceiling act,' a legislative action regulating the size of private properties. The original mansion has been carefully incorporated in an impressive hotel designed lavishly. An excellent example showcasing meaningful work with historic buildings by sponsors and architects.

Second floor rooms courtyards , and suites interiors (below)

Ground and second floor plans

3. Narain Niwas Palace (www.hotelnarainniwas.com)

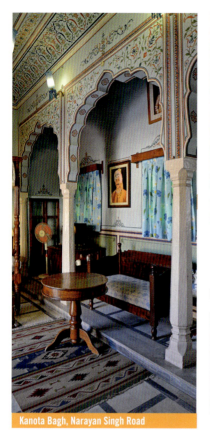

Kanota Bagh, Narayan Singh Road

Although not related to the royal family, the Thakurs of Kanota, an important peripheral settlement, played powerful roles in the princely court. Along with their brothers, who were bestowed the principalities of Santha and Nayla, Kanota's ruling chiefs had migrated from Jodhpur area on the invitation of Sawai Ram Singh. Thakur Amar Singh of Kanota, who ruled from 1924-1942, was both an astute social observer and high-ranking official serving as the commander of Jaipur state army. Writing in English, he kept detailed diaries documenting his worldview and an ethnographic account of princely life. He also built Narain Niwas as a personal retreat in close proximity to the Rambagh palace that had become Maharaja's main residence. An excellent example showcasing Indo-Saracenic style and the prevalent British cultural influence on all aspects of building layout and interior furnishings.

Narain Niwas Palace main facade and entrance area

Rooms furnished with a combination of traditional paintings and colonial furniture

4. Rambagh Palace (www.taj.tajhotels.com)

Bhawani Singh Road, Rambagh

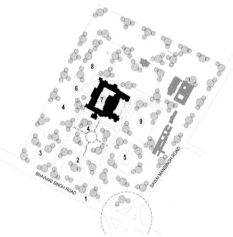

One-of-a-kind of property due to the sheer size, physical settings and interior spaces that conjure romantic nostalgia associated with British-royalty-influenced lifestyle of princely India in the first-half of the 20th century, the Rambagh palace grew from a small garden mansion into a full-fledged garden palace designed by Swinton Jacob in the early 20th century. It advanced further in size and modern amenities while gaining political importance when Jaipur's last Ma-

haraja made Rambagh his main residence in the 1930s. The palace became well-known among party-circuits worldwide due to the famed-hospitality, for celebrity guests hosted by the royal couple—dashing Sawai Man Singh and charming Maharani Gayatri Devi. Following the abolition of princely rule, the Maharaja prudently invited the Taj group, to organize the property's transition into a luxury hotel in 1957, arguably laying the foundation of Jaipur's contemporary hospitality industry.

Passage to the Palace's massive gardens

5. Rajmahal Palace (www.rajmahalpalacejaipur.com)

Sardar Patel Marg, C Scheme

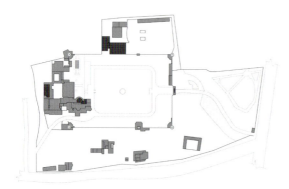

Site plan

Like princely kingdoms elsewhere, the Jaipur state maintained a series of major and minor palaces used a variety of audiences and purposes such as royal entertainment. The phrase *Rajmahal* translates as the King's palace; it was conceived as a garden retreat by Jaipur's founder-king for a favorite queen in the 17th century. Major rebuilding to suit colonial tastes took place around 1820, before it became the official residence of British political agent, who arrived after the signing of an official treaty between the East India company and Jaipur's royal court. Thus, although smaller in size compared to other Jaipur palaces, deeper British influence is visible on building layout and design. Later, the building served as an occasional royal residence and Maharaja's personal guesthouse for the highest-ranking visitors to Jaipur like Queen Elizabeth II.

Palace Hotel gardens, and restaurant and salons at the gallery (above)

6. Hari Mahal Palace (www.harimahalpalace.com)

Tirthraj, Jacob Rd, Civil Lines

Representative interior spaces

Thakurs of Achrol built Hari Mahal Palace as their Jaipur residence near the 'Civil-Lines' area during the 1930s. Civil Lines, a euphemism for the sequestered European quarter in South Asian cities, was a formally-conceived residential settlement of broad streets with bungalows set among vast lots planned by the colonial British during the 19th century. Like elsewhere, Jaipur's Civil Lines housed high-ranking state officials and members of the nobility favored by the Maharaja. Hari Mahal's design derives inspiration from the classical colonial bungalow typology, featuring arcaded verandhas, disciplined spatial geometry with little or no ostentation, and building's modest height but relatively broad mass surrounded by manicured lawns. Notice how Hari Mahal could easily fit into Civil Lines of other Indian cities as well as the city of New Delhi being built around the same time.

7. Taj Jai Mahal Palace (www.taj.tajhotels.com)

Jacob Road, Civil Lines

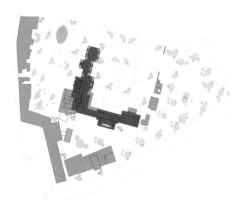

Site plan

The phrase *Jai Mahal* translates as the palace of victory. Following immediately after the City Palace and Rambagh Palace, Jai Mahal occupies an important spot in the hierarchy of royal residences. It began by serving as a modest garden retreat for one of the queen mothers and was later remodeled during the early decades of the XXI century as the official residence for the state's prime minister. Often recruited from outside the princely state, the prime ministers were usually career officials that served as the state's chief executive. They were typically employed both to reduce the Maharaja's burden of governance as well as part of an overall British-promoted effort to modernize the princely administrations. Set among Mughal-style charbagh-pattern landscaped gardens, Jai Mahal offers an excellent example of Indo-Saracenic style official residence repurposed into a luxury five-star palace hotel by the Taj group.

8. Alsisar Haweli (www.alsisarhaveli.com)

SC Road, Shri Ram Colony, Sindhi Camp

Site plan

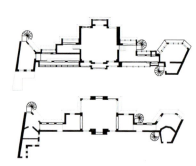

Reception block, first and ground floor plans

Illustrating classical design features of late-19th century townhouse, such as human-scale courtyards and front-lawns and patio, Alsisar Haweli is probably the finest example of careful restoration work and sensitive expansion of the original structure in the entire Rajasthan state. Originally conceived in early 1890s as the Jaipur residence of the Thakurs of Alsisar, the building was repurposed as a modest heritage hotel in the mid-1990s, propitiously just at the beginning of tourism boom. Purposefully-conceptualized incremental expansions, including a swimming pool, additional suites and a *Darbar* hall, using the original design palette and handcrafted stonework have established a widely-emulated template for remodeling heritage properties regionwide. Combining all modern amenities and historic characteristics of a Haveli, this place exemplifies the power of meaningful design.

Representative public spaces

Representative interior spaces

9. Shahpura House (www.shahpura.com)

Devi marg, Bani Park

Ground floor salon, decorated following the traditional styles.

Located 65 km from Jaipur, Shahpura was a principal princely estate ruled by direct descendants of Shekha Ji, a prominent historical figure representing an important offshoot of Jaipur royal family, the Shekhawats. The Thakurs of Shahpura built a colonial-style modern bungalow in the neighborhood developed in the middle of the 20th century. The tourism boom prompted efforts to convert this place, like many others, into a heritage hotel. Borrowing heavily from the historic building palette and employing an eclectic mix of design elements, the builders have completely made-over the colonial-style bungalow to the extent that it represents a new kind of building typology. A prominent example of how contemporary local elites imagine the meaning and purpose of regional building patrimony and employ self-interpretations for remodeling existing properties.

Garden and interior salon

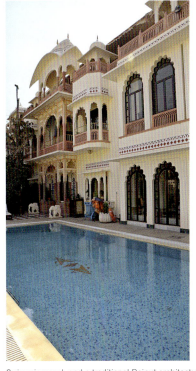

Swimming pool, and a traditional Rajput architecture interior

A. Collectrate Circle Park

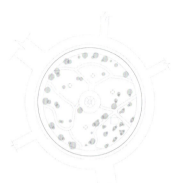

Large roundabout recently landscaped, the Collectorate circle park serves as an important urban node at the intersection of five major streets. Significant public buildings, using dressed-stone masonry and simple geometrical form in a style common for designing civic facilities around the mid-20th century located at all corners.

B. Mathur's Residence

Todar Mal Marg, Bani Park

An excellent example of bungalow-style family-home built during the 1960s. Conceived jointly by an engineer-doctor couple, Mathur's residence provides a glimpse into residential design progressive professionals imagined as an ideal environment to raise a family. Partly repurposed into a guesthouse with owners still-in-residence.

C. Zanana Hospital

Station Road, Sindhi Camp

Front elevation

Ground floor plan

Zanana- Urdu for female- hospital was conceived in the 1920s to focus on women's heathcare, especially the reproductive and child health. Matching the architectural palette of contemporary public buildings (see itinerary V), this civic amenity has continued to serve the original function.

D. Saint Andrews Church - 1872

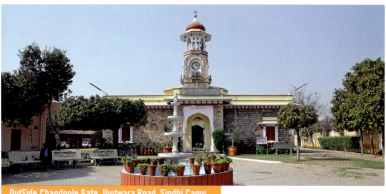

OutSide Chandpole Gate, Jhotwara Road, Sindhi Camp

This is one of the oldest churches in the entire Rajasthan state, sponsored by Maharaja's personal physician Dr. Collin Valentine. One of Jaipur's earliest structures (1872) built with dressed-stone masonry procured from Jhalana hills. Combines classical features of church-design with an interesting spire topped by a *chhatri*.

E. All Saints Church Ar Sir Samuel Swinton Jacob - 1878

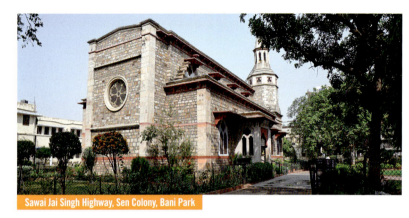

Sawai Jai Singh Highway, Sen Colony, Bani Park

A well-designed church built by Swinton Jacob, who headed the State PWD. He obtained prime land and some support from the Maharaja, while using personal monies to build this elegant church serving Jaipur's tiny Christian community. The building illustrates careful detailing and designer's conception of an Anglican church in India.

F. General Post Office

MI Road

Situated at the important intersection of Sansar Chandra and MI Roads, GPO stands for General Post Office. Designed to showcase the British empire's mighty reach across the Indian subcontinent, GPO buildings are impressive examples of public facilities. Although less important in digital-age, the postal services are still widely-used by the general public.

G. Hotel Khasa Kothi (www.rtdc.in)

MI Road, Gopalbari

Purpose-built as a state guesthouse for important visitors and located strategically close to the Railway station that facilitated flow of visiting tourists from the early 1900s. Taken over by the public-sector and despite inefficient upkeep, Khasa Kothi maintains a certain charm. An excellent example showcasing princely approach to guesthouse design around turn of the 19th century.

H. ITC Rajputana (www.itchotels.in)

Palace Road, Gopalbari

Part of a national chain, and sponsored by the diversified Indian Tobacco Company (ITC Ltd.), this low-height building uses exposed-brick masonry while seeking to interpret regional patrimony across internal spaces.

Starting Point

Birla Mandir

1. Birla Mandir
2. Moti Dungri Fort and Ganesh Temple
3. 72 Screens
4. Sanskrit Bhawan,
   University of Rajasthan
5. Jawahar Kala Kendra (JKK)
6. Jaldhara
7. Malaviya National Institute of Technology
   (MNIT)
8. Jawahar Circle

Additional buildings:

A. Kulish Smriti Van
B. Dr Radhakrishnan Shiksha Sankul

Cafes and Restaurants:

Indian Coffee House

Jawahar Kala Kendra, Jawahar Lal Nehru Marg

Saras Icecream Parlour

Opposite MNIT, JLN Marg, Malviya Nagar

Museums and Arts Centers:

Jawahar Kala Kendra (JKK)

Jawahar Lal Nehru Marg, Opp Commerce College, Jhalana Doongri
www.jkk.artandculture.rajasthan.gov.in

Mool Foundation

67, Mahesh Nagar Phatak, Bajaj Nagar Enclave
www.moolfoundation.in

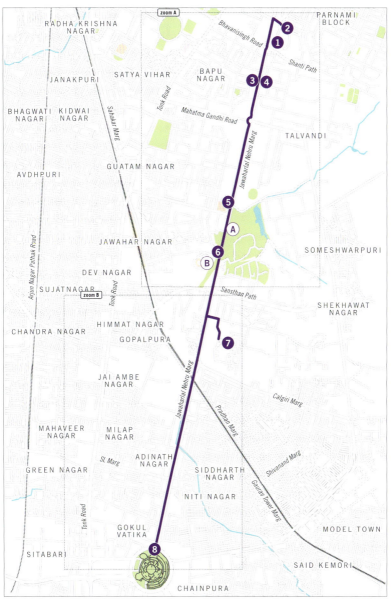

ZOOM A

zoom A

Bhavanisingh Road

Jan Path

Amar Jawan Jyoti

Sawai Mansingh
Stadium

Jaipur
Nagar Nigam

SATYA
VIHAR

GREATER
KAILASH COLONY

Tonk Road

Nehru
Bal Udyan

GUATAM
NAGAR

IPSA

AG COLONY

Mool Foundation

H Taj Rambaug
Palace Hotel

Sawai Mansingh Road

Narayan Singh Road

H Hotel
Narain Niwas
Palace

DOCTOR'S
COLONY

H Grand Uniara
A Heritage Hotel

Reserve Bank of India

Bhavanisingh Road

Jawaharlal Nehru Marg

2 Ganesh Temple
Moti Doongri Fort

1 Birla Mandir

Shanti Path

BAPU NAGAR

3 72 Screens

4 University of
Rajasthan

RAJASTHAN
UNIVERSITY
CAMPUS

Mahatma Gandhi Road

H BLOCK

Mahatma Gandhi Road

BARKET NAGAR
EXTENSION

Jawaharlal Nehru Marg

**Jawahar
Kala Kendra**

Indian Coffee House

5

A Kulish Smriti Van

Jaldhara

6

Dr Radhakrishnan
Shiksha
Bhawan

B

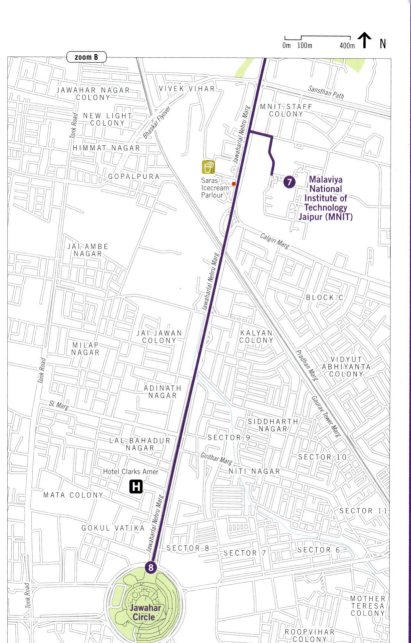

0m 100m 400m ↑ N

JAWAHAR NAGAR COLONY

VIVEK VIHAR

Sansthan Path

MNIT STAFF COLONY

NEW LIGHT COLONY

Tonk Road

Bhaskar Flyover

Jawaharlal Nehru Marg

HIMMAT NAGAR

GOPALPURA

Saras Icecream Parlour

7 Malaviya National Institute of Technology Jaipur (MNIT)

Calgiri Marg

JAI AMBE NAGAR

Jawaharlal Nehru Marg

BLOCK C

JAI JAWAN COLONY

KALYAN COLONY

MILAP NAGAR

Tonk Road

Pradhan Marg

VIDYUT ABHIYANTA COLONY

ADINATH NAGAR

Gaurav Tower Marg

SL Marg

SIDDHARTH NAGAR

LAL BAHADUR NAGAR

SECTOR 9

SECTOR 10

Girdhar Marg

Hotel Clarks Amer

NITI NAGAR

H

MATA COLONY

SECTOR 11

GOKUL VATIKA

Jawaharlal Nehru Marg

SECTOR 8

SECTOR 7

SECTOR 6

Tonk Road

8

MOTHER TERESA COLONY

Jawahar Circle

ROOPVIHAR COLONY

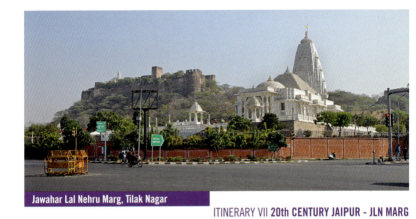

Jawahar Lal Nehru Marg, Tilak Nagar

ITINERARY VII **20th CENTURY JAIPUR - JLN MARG**

ITINERARY LEVEL: Easy (by car)
DURATION: One day
DISTANCE: Around 8 km

PRACTICAL INFORMATION:

All major monuments and museums
are open to the public. See 'Monuments
Timings' p. 210, for details.

Most of the temples are open to the public
from early morning till evening.

JLN (or Jawaharlal Nehru) Marg is the main-street of present-day Jaipur. Connecting the walled city and airport, it traverses mainly through post-independence quarters comprising public buildings and institutional campuses. Its story, however, began with Jaipur's first planned expansion beyond city walls during the late-19th century development of Ram Niwas Bagh campus described in Itinerary V. Subsequent sporadic developments toward the campus's southern edge, such as the building of SMS (Sawai Man Singh) Hospital in 1930s and the Rajasthan University campus during 1940s, catalyzed the building of a connecting road. Then, two developments transformed the road and surrounding land uses.

First, British Raj's partition into independent India and Pakistan in 1947, entailed a large influx of refugees into Jaipur from the nearby regions of Sindh and Punjab

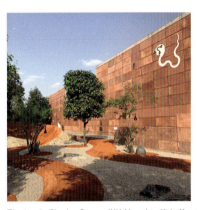

The iconic Charles Correa JKK (Jawahar Kala Kendra) arts center

awarded to Pakistan. Second, from the seat of a relatively-small kingdom, Jaipur became the capital of newly-constituted Rajasthan state founded in early 1950s by the merger of 19 princely states. Shortly-afterwards, the road's development took-off with the building of new neighborhoods like Adarsh Nagar and Gandhi Nagar for refugee populations and Rajasthan's growing bureaucracy, as well as with the many public institutions required by a modern welfare state. Named after India's first Prime-minister, JLN Marg also facilitated Jaipur's outward-oriented development accompanying a slight shift in the city's architectural trajectory even as older preferences and practices continued to persist. Keep this backstory in mind, while exploring JLN Marg as a transect through Jaipur's recent spatial developments exemplifying economic and cultural priorities of 20th century city-builders.

1. **Birla Mandir** B.R. Birla - 1988

Jawahar Lal Nehru Marg, Tilak Nagar

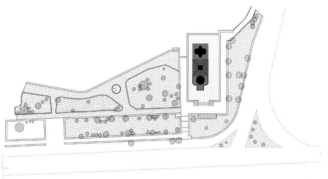

Site plan

Originally from Rajasthan, but headquartered mostly in Kolkata and Mumbai, the Birlas are an important business-house of India, owning several large industries and businesses across the world. Maintaining a largely conservative approach to business-dealings and public-conduct, the Birla family routinely sponsors the building of temples in different Indian cities—always called *Birla Mandir*, or temple—in line with customary expectations from a *Seth*, or traditional businessman, in this part of the world. Built during late 1970s, the temple is sometimes also called Laxmi-Narayan Mandir, after the installed deities. Its building catalyzed a lively debate among the local architectural community about the fit of white temple, built using regionally available marble, against the historic backdrop of Moti Doongri.

The premises also contain a small museum documenting Birlas' family history.

2. Moti Dungri Fort and Ganesh Temple

Jawahar Lal Nehru Marg, Tilak Nagar

Site plan

A series of military forts and outposts watched over Jaipur's periphery. A small fort called Shankargarh existed at this strategic location. Sawai Man Singh II upgraded this building during the 1930s into a petite palace. The colonists had sent the young Maharaja to the UK during formative years both for keeping him away from court-intrigues and grooming him in the image of a British gentleman. Thus, not surprisingly, *Moti Doongri* (translates as 'pearl hill') reminds you of a Scottish castle. The Moti Doongri temple dedicated to *Ganesh Ji* (the 'elephant god') began modestly around the turn of 19th century. Ganesh Bhagwan is the remover of obstacles in the Hindu tradition and, thus, customarily evoked at the beginning of any enterprise. Try to visit on a Wednesday, traditionally seen as Ganesh Ji's day, when people bring brand-new cars and two-wheelers straight from the showrooms for his blessings.

JLN Marg, Opp Rajasthan University

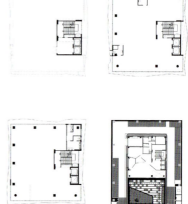

Plans (clockwise): terrace, fifth, ground and third floor plans

Located across the Rajasthan University campus, the building stands out in provocative contrast with the public-sector's conventional design approach. Conceived like a simple cube covered with 72 precast screens organized geometrically as 'outer skin.' The emphatically-prominent screens make a symbolic reference to *Jaalis* in the manner used by architect Raj Rewal for designing the much-acclaimed 'hall of nations' inaugurated 1972 at the Pragati Maidan, Delhi. *Jaalis* were traditionally employed in this region due to the wide availability of workable stone, cultural privacy concerns, and climatic conditions (*Jaalis* scatter the glare, allowing-in tolerable sunlight while facilitating passive ventilation). However, this building also exemplifies the notion of 'foot-loose architecture' and the ongoing search for 'contemporary global,' evident in many parts of the world including India.

4. Sanskrit Bhawan, University of Rajasthan

Jawaharlal Nehru Marg, Rajasthan University Campus, Jhalana Doongri

The Sanskrit Bhawan building on top; above courtyard views from another campus building

Situated opposite Birla Mandir, Sanskrit Bhawan marks the northeastern edge of Rajasthan university's campus founded in 1940s. Launched during Mirza Ismail's premiership, this is the first and largest university in the entire state. Built just a few years ago by university's inhouse engineers at this strategic location, Sanskrit Bhawan is an important building symbolizing the continuation of a rather conservative streak in city's architectural and educational traditions.

This is so because the Jaipur kings promoted Jaipur as 'Chotti Kashi,' or 'mini Varanasi,' this being the city reputed for Sanskrit learning in ancient India. The use of dressed-stone masonry and simple geometry of building form, similar to many older civic and public buildings described in Itinerary V, exemplifies the continuing influence of public-sector's traditional building practices.

5. Jawahar Kala Kendra Ar. Charles Correa - 1983

Jawaharlal Nehru Marg, Jhalana Doongri

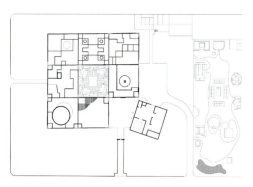

Site plan

Perhaps the most well-known architectural project built in post-independence Jaipur. Popularly-known as JKK, this a cultural center named after India's first Prime-Minister Jawaharlal Nehru. In line with Nehru's ideal of building a modern nation while retaining the meaningful spiritual essence of an ancient country, JKK's design aims to combine insights from Jaipur's architectural patrimony and the region's rich cultural traditions within the ambit of Correa's life-long project of seeking a suitable architecture for contemporary India. In this sense, Correa's design approach to JKK cannot be understood without a brief foray into his overall architectural oeuvre.

A prominent member of Independent India's first generation of architects, Correa was trained in the US during the early 1950s when modernism was both dominant as an architectural style and perceived as a universal solution to multiple problems of the postwar world. Not surprisingly, some of his

Courtyard open-to-sky on top; above inside and outisde images of the dome containing a cosmic painting

earliest projects, like the Portuguese Church in Mumbai, reflect the deep-modernist influence even as much of his work, like the Bharat Bhawan at Bhopal, illustrate the search for an Indian idiom articulating the modernist impulse.

Conceived during the 1980s, JKK stands out for three distinct features. First, the building form and layout explicitly encapsulate Jaipur's city plan and spatial organization like a self-contained microcosm. The building nei-ther refers to the surroundings nor interacts with the adjoining structures, just like an internally-oriented traditional Haveli or Palace. Second, notice Correa's characteristically careful detailing, ranging from the entrance ramp off the JLN Marg to purposefully-select-ed frescos and cleverly-placed open-to-sky courtyards. Finally, true to the purpose, JKK successfully connects city's youth and visiting tourists to diverse cultural events taking place around-the-year.

6. Jaldhara

Gandhi Nagar

Site plan

Jal means water, and *Dhara* means a stream, so *Jal-Dhara* translates as water-stream. Conceived as a linear parkway running parallel to a manmade water channel in early 2000s and together with the nearby wide-open campus of Shiksha Sankul, later-described Kulish Smiriti Van, and an older public-park called Mahaveer Udyan, Jaldhara constitutes a city-level green space comprising a variety of open spaces and recreational areas. Importantly, the development of these places represent a growing civic consciousness among the city's general population and local authorities. The combination of India's growing economy, which fuels the prosperity of higher and middle classes, and the deteriorating quality of city life has catalyzed the development of parks, open spaces and recreational areas across urban India.

7. Malaviya National Institute of Technology Jaipur (MNIT)

Jhalana Gram, Malviya Nagar

Site plan

Originally designed by an ardent-modernst, and one of Independent India's leading architect, Achyut Kanvinde in 1960s, MNIT is a regionally-significant institution dedicated largely to the study of engineering but also comprises Rajasthan state's first public school of architecture. The campus is deeply-modernist in spatial organization and architectural character employing a mix of exposed concrete and random-rubble masonry using locally-available stone. The campus developed in two distinct phases: Main administrative block and surrounding buildings including the architecture department built per Kanvinde's proposals (where you can still feel the spirit of original design); and the more recent buildings designed by assorted architects including those from the engineering-oriented Central Public Work Department (CPWD).

8. Jawahar Circle

Site plan

Jawahar Circle, Malviya Nagar

Jawahar Circle is both a large roundabout as well as a relatively new public-park. It is part of the larger city-level green infrastructure comprising multiple parks and open spaces that the authorities have begun developing in recent years. It also serves as a crucial transport node connecting several important intra-city highways and city roads to the JLN Marg.

A. Kulish Smriti Van

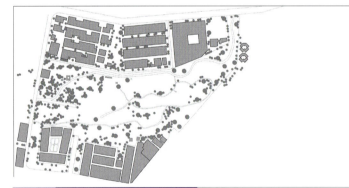

Site plan

Jawahar Lal Nehru Marg, Bajaj Nagar

Kulish Smriti Van is a newly-established nature reserve comprising differently-landscaped areas representing regional bio-diversity (also played an important role supporting intensive plantation to prevent further land erosion in this flood-prone area). It celebrates the memory of Karpoor Chandra Kulish, who founded the Rajasthan Patrika newspaper.

B. Dr Radhakrishnan Shiksha Sankul

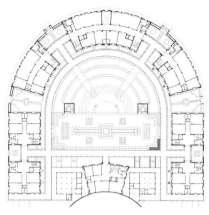

Ground floor plan

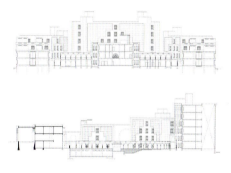

Sections and elevation

Designed during early 2000s, by then locally prominent firm Aayojan Architects, this campus brings together many departments and agencies dealing with the field of education. Organized around a central courtyard, the coherently conceived cluster of institutional buildings extends public-sector's rather conservative approach to public buildings via clever designing. Conceived as a self-financed project, where part of the land was auctioned to raise monies for developing the campus, Shiksha Sankul exemplifies state's increasingly proactive approach toward resource mobilization.

Jaipur (जयपुर) is both the capital and largest city of the state of Rajasthan situated in Northwestern India. Sawai Jai Singh II, the ruler of Amer which was the historic capital of this region, founded Jaipur as a brand-new city based on a formal plan conceived in 1727. Seven main gateways in the perimeter wall control access to the city that centers on the City Palace. The gridiron layout creates nine blocks, called chowkdis, or squares, of approximate 800 meters X 800 meters. Each chowkdi serves as a socio-spatial neighborhood comprising both residential units and commercial areas that many visitors like touring. Public amenities and major bazaars abut main intersecting roads. But walking on inner streets provides a closer view of Jaipur's unique urbanity that the many generation of residents have created over time.

Beyond the historic center, some of the major neighborhoods popular among tourists are: C Scheme, Bani Park, M.I. Road, Bapu Nagar, Tilak Nagar, Raja Park, Malviya Nagar and Vaishali Nagar. Some visitors also like Mansarovar and Vidyadhar Nagar situated about six kilometers from the central city. Majority of city hotels are located in and around Bani park, Sindhi Camp area, C Scheme and Malviya Nagar. Commercial areas and shopping districts dominate Jaipur's land use. See Itinerary III for famous bazaars and shopping areas located in city's historical center.

WHEN TO GO

Geographically, Jaipur is located on the eastern-side of the Aravalli range of mountains, just beyond which lies the Thar desert. Jaipur's climate is semi-arid, comprising three main seasons: a dry temperate winter (October-March), warm summer (April-July) and a brief but intense rainy period during the monsoon season (August-September). The winters are typically bearable, but summers are substantially warm. So, prepare accordingly.

Tourists usually visit Jaipur and nearby places during winters, and the best time to visit is between November and February. Early Mornings are typically the best time to visit buildings and places. Although day-long excursions are usually required for heritage walks, water walks, and local religious and cultural festivals encapsulating regional lifestyle and social practices. Photographs tend to come out best in the early morning hours, though dusk offers its own qualities.

The summer is hot and dry, making it difficult to walk or bike long-distances. The average temperature is around 33 °C (91.4 °F) but can easily reach up to 45 °C (113 °F) during peak season. However, one can still undertake heritage walks, adventure tours, water walks and architectural tours offered by tour operators and local architects in early mornings or late afternoons. Carrying cool water, using sunscreen and wearing comfortable shoes, light cotton clothing, sunglasses and a hat or cap is always a good idea.

If traveling between December and mid March, please keep in mind that the diurnal temperature difference can be quite high

So, while it might be cold during nights and early morning, it can become quite warm during the day. Therefore, pack accordingly combining woolens as well as cotton clothes.

HOW TO REACH

 Air

Jaipur has a busy 'international airport,' receiving mostly domestic flights, located about 13 kilometers from the city center at the southern suburb of Sanganer. The nearest truly international airport is the Indira Gandhi International Airport (IGI) located at Gurgaon in the Delhi region. Alternately, you can also fly into Mumbai, Ahmedabad, Chennai and Bangalore and take directly connecting flights to Jaipur.

From IGI's International Terminal (T3) you can easily transfer to the domestic terminal from where some of the major Indian airlines operate flights to Jaipur (Air India, Jet Airways, Vistara, Spice Jet Airlines, Indigo, GoAir and more). Keep in mind that you may have to transfer (via a shuttle) from the International Terminal (T3) to Domestic Terminal (T2) that can take about an hour. There are about twenty daily flights between IGI and Jaipur available through-out the day. Flights take about 55 minutes and can cost between $20 to $250 each way, depending on the traveling season and how far in advance you book. Jaipur airport also offers direct flights to many nearby places and faraway cities such as: Bikaner, Kota, Jodhpur, Banaras, Agra, Dehradun, Lucknow, Kochi, Goa, Udaipur, Kolkatta, Pune, Hyderabad, Srinagar, Chandigarh and Dehradun. Always a good idea to check latest updates to flight schedules.

 Train

The most economical way to reach Jaipur from Delhi and other Indian cities is by train. Currently, there are six trains daily between New Delhi Railway Station and Jaipur while the number of weekly connections is as high as 23. The fastest train between Delhi and Jaipur is called the 'Rajdhani Express' that takes just under four and a half hours. 'Jaipur Double-Decker' and the 'Shatabdi Express' are perhaps the most popular options taking about the same time. Reserved seats can be booked at the main railway station or online (by Indian tourists only), till four hours prior to the train departure.

You can also make train reservations from several other Railway stations in Jaipur and from the Sindhi Camp Bus Stand. There are also several 'Sampark Kendras' and 'e-mitra centers' located all across Jaipur, which also offer train-booking facilities. Another option is to visit a travel agency. You can also book train tickets online on the Indian Railway's website (www.indianrail.gov.in). However, the website only accepts payments by credit cards issued in India, and thus may not be a good choice for international tourists, although you can view information regarding train schedules.

Direct trains to-and-fro from Jaipur to Jaisalmer, Bikaner, Jodhpur, Agra, Kota are also available. These journeys take about three to seven hours with express/mail trains. Highly recommended to book tickets if you want to take a long trip or are traveling on specific dates, since the railways is not only the most-used transport system for mid to long distance trips in India but also because people usually book tickets well in advance. Good idea to book tickets in the Chair car, or air conditioned coaches (CC,

1AC, 2AC and 3AC) because they are relatively more comfortable. Although during the winter months, it is okay to take short journeys in second class without air conditioning.

The train station is situated about 13 Kilometers from the airport and you can take prepaid taxis, bus, Ola or Uber cabs or autorickshaw (Tuk-tuk).

Taxi

You can make the journey to Jaipur from Delhi by taxi, which is perhaps the most convenient but also the most expensive option. This offers no advantage over bus or train if you're not in a rush and if you are travelling alone or with just one other person. The journey will take about the same time and, remember, roads-accidents in India are frequent and often fatal.

However, if in a group of 3-4 persons or carrying substantial luggage, you may prefer to take a taxi from Delhi Airport. Advisable to hire one from the prepaid counter located at the terminal's exit. You can also hire a taxi from the hotel you are staying in. However, it's always advisable to agree on a fixed price before starting the journey and usually, it is more economic to use the prepaid counters that can also be found in the train station in Delhi.

With apps like Uber and Ola inter-city travel has become lot easier, specially for national tourists. There are also taxi sharing options available with predefined pick up and drop points; though this is comparatively a cheaper option but safety remains a concern.

HOW TO GET AROUND IN THE CITY

Although English is the language of administration, and what you will see on most bus markings and traffic signs, bus and rickshaw drivers speak it just barely and it's not often beyond numbers and some basic words. However, feel free to ask around as the people are very welcoming and helpful. Many typically reach out, ensuring that you are on the right track to reach your destination.

Bus

Another feasible option to reach Jaipur from Delhi International Airport terminal (T3) is to take the popular 'Volvo Bus' operated by the Rajasthan State Road Transport Corporation (RSRTC). The service begins at Sarai Kale Khan interstate bus terminus but also picks passengers from Dhola Kuan and IFFCO chowk on the way to Jaipur. You can take the Delhi airport Metro train to Dhola Kuan or a taxi to IFFCO chowk. The journey to Jaipur takes about five hours and buses are available at regular interval from five in the morning until after midnight. Private transport agencies also run buses from Fatehpuri in old Delhi via Dhaula Kaun, IIFCO chowk and IGI Airport to Jaipur.

For traveling to Delhi from Jaipur, you can book tickets at the RSRTC booking center at Narain Singh Circle or the main bus stand called Sindhi Camp. You can also book tickets online from the RSRTC website up to two hours before departure, or even buy the ticket directly, arriving half an hour before departure. Private travel agencies running bus services are located in proximity of the main railway station and the central bus stand, Sindhi Camp, Jaipur.

The main bus terminal (Inter State) is located at Sindhi Camp, a place to catch a bus to almost anywhere in the city including the outskirts of the city as well. The station operates in two areas – local buses as well as intercity buses (always confirm with the bus driver). One can also get buses for inter city commuting. One can also get frequent buses for close by tourist spots and cities like Bundi, Kota, Ajmer, Sikar, Delhi, Dehradun, Bikaner, Dausa, etc.

Although at first glance it seems complicated to get familiar with the bus network in the city and even more difficult as it may result in some cases to find the stops, the city has an extensive network of buses and can get you most places. With a little prior communication with the bus driver and conductors you can find your destinations easily. Some of the main lines also have A.C. charted buses.

 Rickshaw

These are the most popular means of transport in the city (and in the country), and although foreign visitors sometimes get the feeling that they're being charged more money, it's worth taking a few minutes to agree on a price and use them to get around the city.

Apart from the stops that can be found next to the shopping centre areas in the city, and in the Walled City, you can also find them near the most frequented buildings like institutions, large housing societies, important roads like MI Road, JLN Road, Sikar Road, Agra Road, hospitals or universities, and use them to get around to many places.

The rates depend on the distance and the best way to move around in walled city is e-rickshaws which are shared by six people

at a time and charge a fixed Rs. 10/- for decided destinations. One can also take a cycle rickshaw to move around in the walled city that can cater to 2-3 people at a time. Here too, it is a good idea to spare some time to fix the rates before starting the travel.

To avoid surprises in the fares one can also use an app called 'Jugnoo', for ease in getting autorickshaws and also to get minimum fixed fare according to your destination. This is also a good option to travel during early winter mornings.

THE BASICS

 ATMs

While most of the bigger restaurants will accept major credit cards and debit cards, cash is still the dominant form of payment. The city has a multitude of ATM machines, that accept most major international debit cards and are spread across all areas, usually in and around the major commercial areas, institutions and healthcare institutions. It is often easier to use a debit card to withdraw money than to use a credit card.

Hotels usually require a fee to use credit cards, and some stores may ask for it as well, though it is not usual.

Paytm and Bheem are widely used apps for cash transfer using mobile number or bar code to encourage plastic cash; these can be refilled by using credit or debit cards. Both can be easily downloaded on one's phone from play store on any Android or iOS operating systems with an active internet connection.

Business Hours

Government offices and public institutions usually open between 10:00am to 5:00pm from Monday to Friday and from 10:00 am to 2:00 pm on 1st and 3rd Saturdays.

Shopping areas and commercial districts typically open between 10:00 am and 8-9 pm. And most of the shopping areas are open on Sundays as well; the shops in walled city though remain shut on the day.

Holidays and Festivals

India has two National Holidays that all institutional offices and buildings, shops and attractions follow, although transport is not affected during that time. There are Republic Day (26th January) and Independence Day (15th August).

There are also innumerable religious festivals which are more famous than national holidays like, Dussehra between September-October, Diwali between October November and Holi between Feburary-March. These festivals are celebrated by people from all region across the country.

The best time to visit Jaipur coincides with these festivals and the best time is during Diwali, the Festival of Lights or Vijaydashmi. If you visit the city during Vijay Dashmi or Dusshera, one can witness the Ram Leela, performed for ten days at the Ram Leela Maidan followed by the destruction of the evil Raavana's towering effigies with fireworks celebrating victory of God Ram over the evil and also marking the preparations for Diwali celebrations. Diwali is celebrated by decorating all the buildings with earthen divas or lights for at least a week's time and that's a sight to behold.

From January till March there are a lot of local festivals that are celebrated in Jaipur and all across Rajasthan like 'Makar Sankranti' on 14th January, more famous as the kite festival of Jaipur. The tourism department organizes a Kite flying festival for the locals as well as the international tourists.

If you want to visit Jaipur during Feburary, one can attend the Jaipur Literature Festival, some of the international book events and towards the end of February- Holi, the festival of colours that can be celebrated with the locals. The celebrations last for a week at Govind Dev Ji temple.

If one wishes to visit Jaipur in mid-March, Gangaur, a local festival celebrated by married women can be witnessed. There takes place a grand and royal progression of clay Gangauri's of the royal family, from Tripolia Bazaar till City Palace, Jaipur. Further information and tickets are available on the Rajasthan tourism website. March 31st is celebrated as Rajasthan Foundation day when celebrations for different age-groups and varying cultural interests take place at different locations of the city; updates regarding these are made available on the Rajasthan tourism website.

Few more festivals that are celebrated in the walled city are -Ramadaan- a one month celebration in Muslim community and during which a temporary night market comes up for a month in Ramganj Mandi.

These festivals are based on Lunar calendar and the dates may vary. It is advisable to refer to the Rajasthan tourism website for the updated information about the festival dates and the celebrations, before doing the final bookings.

@ Internet

Most of the hotels and restaurants have wifi facility and the password is available on request. There are also a few areas where one can find free Jionet wifi hotspots: these are in and around Bani park, Gandhi Nagar railway station, Jawahar Kala Kendra, C Scheme, Civil Lines, MI Road, Vidyadhar Nagar, Badi Choupad, Bhawani Singh Road, Vaishali Nagar, Element Mall Ajmer Road, Shyam Nagar, Sodala, Gujjar ki Thadi, Gopalpura Byepass, Jawahar Circle, Murlipura, Jhotwara, Agra Road and even the Vishwakarma Industrial Area. There are few internet cafes located within the Walled City and one can also find internet facilities at print shops.

Language

The official languages are Hindi and English, a few fringe and peri urban areas have Marwari speaking population as well. The administrative language is English so you will find all the information and instructions in English. Even though the streets and the shops signages are mostly in Hindi, English has become more popular among the younger generations. The most widely used language is Hindi but the people can manage to communicate in English as well.

Medical Assistance

The major government hospital is the Sawai Man Singh medical college and hospital, located on JLN Marg. You can find private practices all across the city and there are a few speciality hospitals as well along with some private hospitals catering to the medical needs of the residents and close by peri urban and rural areas. Mahatma Gandhi Hospital, Naraina Multi Speciality, Fortis, Soni Hospital, Santokba Durlabhji,

Jaipur Hospital, Monilek, Apex hospital, Calgiri Hospital, to name a few.

Pharmacies

You can find pharmacies close to the hospitals as well as in all the commercial areas of the city. These shops have a good collection of personal care and grooming products as well.

$ Money

The rupee is the official currency of India-you can change US Dollars, Euros and most other currencies in banks (the vast majority are in and around Statue Circle, Malviya Nagar, C Scheme, Jai Singh Highway, and commercial areas) and in money exchange offices.

i Tourist Information

There are tourist information kiosks located at the Bus stand, railway station and the airport. The main tourist office is located at MI road, and there are branches at the major RTDC hotels like hotel Gangaur, hotel Khasa Kothi, hotel Teej, hotel Swagatam. RTDC information kiosks are located at major tourist spots in and around walled city. There are also RTDC authorised shops where one can find relevant information. Apart from these places you can also approach the traffic police help desks all across the city at major roads of the city.
For more information you can access the official city web page (http://tourism.rajasthan.gov.in)

WC Toilets

There are 'Sulabh Shauchalayas' (toilets and bathrooms) constructed in each and every locality whether commercial, tourist spots, public areas, bus stand, major bus stops, railway stations, airport, etc. These services are priced between Rs 4/- to Rs10/- depending on the facilities that one wants to avail. These are maintained toilets with provision of basic amenities. You can also find toilets constructed at petrol pumps. This facility has made road travel very convenient and also desirable.

TOURIST BUSES

There are five daily tours conducted by RTDC: one full day tour, three half day tours and one evening tour- Pink City by night (with dinner) to see the important buildings of Jaipur. These tours have a pick up location at railway station as well as the main bus stand. Tickets can be purchased at RTDC offices as well as on-line bookings are also available. It is advisable to book them in advance as the seats fill up fast.

Places to eat

Rajasthan is famous for its rich delicacies, from street stalls to grand restaurants. The cuisine is varied and serves to the tastes of people from all across the globe. Apart from the local Rajasthani food, Punjabi, South-Indian, Chinese, Thai, Mexican, Italian and American fast food is also widely available now. Multiple major food chains from across the world have an outlet in the city. Apart from the restaurants, mithai or sweet shops are very famous where you can try a large variety of local desserts and namkeens- spicy savory snacks.

There are Saras cafes where one can have a quick breakfast located at some major

roads of the city like JLN Marg and near the Secretariat and SKIT, etc. One can also opt to have a quick breakfast at the Indian Coffee House located at Jawahar Kala Kendra or at the outlet on MI Road. Other options are the local sweet shops in the commercial areas of the walled city.

One can try different local freshly prepared snacks like samosa, mawa kachori, pyaaz ki kachori, kanji bada and sweets like kesar ghewar, Rabri ghewar, phini, gujhiya, jalebi, rasgullas etc. A few of the famous shops are Rawat Mishthan Bhandar, Kanji Sweets, Doodh Mishthan Bhandar, Sodhani Sweets, Lakshmi Mishthan Bhandar, Kanha, Bikanerwala, etc.
The dhabas are also a good option and a few of the top vegetarian choices are Sharma Dhaba on Sikar Road and RJ 14 on Ajmer Road.

Among the theme restaurants Chokhi Dhaani is a must visit. Located on the outskirts of Jaipur, one experiences here a rural setup to experience along with a traditional meal called dal bati and churma with few other delicacies. One can also visit Viraat Restaurant, on Sahkaar Marg if a central location is preferred. There is also a tea cafe and restaurant called Tapri where you can taste as many as at least 50 varieties of tea, with some other alternatives.

There are also a wide variety of places where you can choose to eat and many of them are located in and around Sindhi Camp and the railway station. If you go to Bani Park, MI road or C Scheme one can find almost all variety and ranges of food options, Bani Park has higher range of restaurants a few are really interesting like Peacock restaurant, NIBS Cafe, Jaipur Adda, Bottle Chimney or the Forresta. Civil

Lines also has a high end mixed variety of food options available a few of them Spice Court, Taruveda Organic Cafe and Cinnamon are good choices.

However MI road, Malviya Nagar and C Scheme has a mix range of places to opt for. A few to name are Suryamahal, Copper Chimney, Handi, Om Revolving tower on MI Road are some other good options. A few more choices for food and drinks are Anokhi Cafe, The Rajput room, Zolocrust, Samode Haveli, 1135 AD, Bar Palladio, House of people, Black Out, Reza, etc.

H Places to stay

Most of the hotels in town are located in and around Sindhi Camp, Polo Victory areas, close to the railway station and the bus stand. Many have also been located in the walled city that are havelis converted into guest houses or hotels. Luxurious and elegant palaces that have also been turned into hotels and are located in the nearby rural areas.

In the past few years a lot of development has taken place to encourage different tourism options in the city. This has resulted in a large variety of staying options to fulfil varying requirements of tourists visiting the city. There are a lot of properties that have come up in the posh areas near the airport, although these places are not very popular with the tourists on leisure trips rather with those who are on work trips.

There are a lot of websites that provide support for staying options like trivago.com, airbnb.co.in, oyo.com. One can get good deals on these websites or try getting a deal in person at the hotel. You can also choose to do the bookings via travel agents and opt for packages.

There are a lot of options available for stay in other facilities like RSRTC hotels, youth hostels, private hotels, traditional havelis or houses converted into accommodations, backpackers hostels, etc. These options range from cheaper to midlevel to luxurious accommodations. If you are booking the accommodation online it is advised to read the customer reviews available on the portal. It would also be better if you don't rely entirely on the pictures provided on the Internet and get in touch with the hotel management staff before confirming your bookings.

According to the ratings and ,the reviews based on pricing, services and basic amenities, a few of the establishments have been described at Itinerary , and in addition others also listed below.

3* rating: Hotel Red Fox (JLN Marg), Hotel surya Villa, Krishna Palace, Ibis Jaipur, Arya Niwas, Regenta Central (Jal Mahal), Umaid residency, Sarovar Portico, Devraj Niwas, Naila Bagh Palace, Umaid Bhawan Heritage House, Achrol House, The Pearl Palace.

4* rating: Hotel Diggi Palace, Samode Haveli, HariMahal Palace, Four Points by Sheraton, Hotel Ashok, Shahpura House, The Fern, Radisson Blu, Park Prime, Alsisar Haveli, Holiday Inn, Hotel Royal Orchid, Golden tulip, Chokhi Dhani, Hotel Narain Niwas, Dera Mandawa.

5* rating: The Lalit, Jaipur Marriott, Clark's Amer, The Rambagh Palace, Taj Jai Mahal Palace, Hotel Trident, Hotel Taj SMS, Hotel ITC Rajputana, The Hilton, The Oberoi Rajvillas, Lebua Resort, Hotel Ramada, The Raj Palace, Taj Mahal palace and Sujan Rajmahal Palace.

Markets and shops

The shopping options in Jaipur are overwhelming in variety. The walled city of Jaipur is famous for exquisite intricate Gold and silver jewelry, antique furniture, traditional home furnishings including artefacts, carpets, blue pottery etc, local Sanganeri prints in fabric and dresses, handbags, bed sheets, famous cotton blankets, perfumes, books, mojaries, leather crafted wallets, belts, Zardosi and Gota work garments etc. Most of the shops within the walled city are wholesale suppliers but one can also find retailers with the same pricing options.

The Walled city is planned in such a way that the major commercial areas are located along the primary and secondary roads and every tertiary road has a specific assigned bazaar. If we start from MI road, there are many shops for exclusive Gold jewelry, one of the oldest jewelry stores – 'The Gem Palace' can be visited for expensive traditional jewelry. MI Road has a famous lassi wala -a local sweetened yogurt drink, bangle shops and a wide range of western brands, etc.

MI Road will further take you towards the Ajmeri Gate (marking one of the seven entrance gateways to the walled city) from where the main market area starts. Starting from Nehru Bazaar famous for trinkets, clothes and perfumes, Bapu Bazaar is thronged for buying traditional jewelry, handicrafts, bags, clothes, and the local handicrafts. Johri Bazaar is another market famous for jewelry including the traditional gem works, Sterling silver jewelry, antique jewelry, and similar collections. The area outside Hawa Mahal also has a lot of shopping options available varying from traditional leather footwear, to local Sanganeri print dresses, leather bags, handicrafts, handcrafted lamps, blue pottery etc. There is a vegetables and fruit market here as well.

Specific bazaars and streets are reserved for particular products and famous for specific businesses. Tripolia market has lots of bicycle shops, hardware and gardening tools shops, and utensil outlests, Lalji Saand Ka Rasta is famous for sarees, Thhathheron Ka Rasta is famous for steel utensils and Link Road for bed sheets and dresses and footwear shops. For trying local cuisines and fried snacks Ghee Walon Ka Rasta is a one stop shop. Uday singh Ji ki Haveli houses shops for toiletries and birthday party and stationery supplies at wholesale prices. Chaura Rasta is famous for bookstores that have books for general reading, competition preparation and for schools. Sitapura apparel park is a place where you can get ready made garments in wholesale prices. Atish Market is known for hardware and sanitary ware stores.

Other than the walled city, some of the major commercial areas include Mansarovar main market, Sindhi Colony market, Shashtri Nagar, Bagadia Bhawan (C Scheme), Satkar market and Kardhani market in Malaviya nagar, Raja Park central fashion street, Jawahar Nagar, Sahkar Marg, Lal Kothi, GT, Janta Stores (Babu Nagar).

The central fruits and vegetable are located at village Muhana and Lal Kothi. Other than these there are also weekly farmer markets held on regular basis on different days at different locations and are very famous.

There are also guided tours that one can take to watch the local craftsmen work on the traditional Zardosi embroidery, Gota Patti, Kinari, silver ornaments, Lac bangles and precious and semi precious stones in Johri Bazaar and Badi Chaupar Area.

There are also many malls that have come up and one can definitely visit them for access to a wide range of western brands. But if you wish to get to know the city, it's history and it's culture the best option is to explore the local markets in the walled city. However, the new establishments are very popular among the locals and if you wish to quench your curiosity you can visit a few of the famous malls, like WTP (Jawahar circle) which has outlets of many international and national brands, a giant food court and a multiplex cinema; or Gaurav Tower (GT) that has both local and branded stuff along with lots of food kiosks.

Bookshops Libraries and Maps

Some of the best stores are located in the central area of the city. Universal Books on MI road is also one of the oldest bookstores in Jaipur and has a large collection of general books as well as city guides and maps of India. One can also visit Book World, located in the Rajasthan University campus and Crossword (C Scheme) or BAGS (Hawa Sadak, Civil Lines).

Om Shanti OSHO library, Jawahar Kala Kendra Library and the Central Library at Rajasthan University have extensive catalogues and good reading areas.

EXCURSIONS AROUND JAIPUR

With Jaipur as headquarters, you can take many short trips for a few days or use it as a good starting point to explore the culturally rich and colorful state of Rajasthan. There are many cities to visit from Jaipur, at varying distances, however a few of the must visit places are Udaipur, Jaisalmer, Bikaner, Mount Abu, Jodhpur, Ajmer, Fatehpur Sikri, Alwar, Shekhawati cities, etc. One must at least keep 10 days aside to tour through Rajasthan. Other than these cities there are also a few more places of architectural or historical importance where one can plan a day's trip. One can hire a taxi and visit these places; frequent public transportation is also available.

ABHANERI

Abhaneri town is just 95 kms away from Jaipur. The Harshat Mata temple here is considered to be the temple of Goddess of Joy and Happiness and believed to have spread the joy to the whole village. It is also known for its unique architecture and amazing craftsmanship that dates back to Medieval India. Chand Baori belongs to

10th century monuments displaying Rajasthani architectural skills and talents. It is huge well with flights of steps on the three sides leading to the water reserve. With 13 levels and a depth of 20 meter, Chand Baori, a colossal step well is located just in front of the famous Harshat Mata temple.

BAGRU
Bagru is a small but very famous village for its unmatchable age old tradition of wooden block printing. 'Bagru prints' are quite a brand as the unique wooden printing technique makes them a class apart.

BHANGARH
Bhangarh is located in the Rajgarh tehsil of the district Alwar and is just 88 kms from the city of Jaipur. Built by one of Akbar's "Navratan"- Jaipur's Raja Man Singh Ji for his grandson, all the buildings in the Bhangarh fort now only can be seen as ruins. Most have suffered collapsed roofs except the temple. Bhangarh is said to be haunted and this adds to its charm!

CHOMU
Chomu is a Rajasthani village famous for its heritage havelis richly ornamented with paintings and is on the Sikar highway. It has a 300 year old elegant palace known as 'Chomu Palace'; this is a must visit.

RAMGARH LAKE
Ramgarh Lake is a very famous tourist attraction, especially during monsoon when it is filled with water. It has marvelous scenic beauty with and is a special attraction for the wildlife lovers as in its vicinity is the Ramgarh Wildlife Sanctuary.

SAMBHAR LAKE
Sambhar Lake is also popularly known as 'Salt Lake of Rajasthan' as it is a source of large amount of salt production. Spread over 22.5 km area, this is India's largest inland salt lake and is regarded as a 'Gift from Thar desert'.

SAMODE PALACE
The palace is 33 kms north west of Jaipur and can be reached by public transportation till Chandwaji. Exclusive and discreet, Samode Palace has been host to royalty, celebrities, artists, and the discerning traveler. It is one of the finest example of Indo-Saracenic architecture in India.

SANGANER
Sanganer is famous for its handmade block prints called 'Sanganeri prints' that are unique to this town, along with the blue pottery.

SARISKA
Sariska is a Tiger reserve established by the government of India and is about 107 kms from Jaipur. Spread across 866 sq kms with the Aravalli range in the background, Sariska offers exuberant natural beauty and great bio diversity.

TONK
Tonk is a town, situated on the banks of the River Banas in the Tonk district of Rajasthan. It is located at a distance of 95 km from the city of Jaipur and a heritage site. On the way to Tonk is Banasthalli Vidhyapeeth, one of the early pre-independence educational institutions dedicated to encouraging education of the girl child. The institution offers graduate degrees in vocational and professional courses.

VIRAT NAGAR
Virat Nagar or the very recent Bairat, is one of the northern most towns of Jaipur district. Located on the Delhi – Alwar highway, the town is situated 52 km from Jaipur. It is famous for relics and structures of Mauryan, Mughal and Rajput periods.

VIDYADHAR NAGAR
B.V. DOSHI (VSF) - 1984

*While planning planning Vidyadhar Nagar,
how can we ignore what Maharaja Jaisingh
contemplated while planning the city of Jaipur? Few fundamentals and the city of Jaipur becomes a paradise on earth. To create
a paradise one must be happy, healthy and
must live well; to live well, one must have
opportunities, skills and knowledge; to provide employment there has to be markets
and useful products; to maintain and grow
one must pay taxes and to pay taxes - one
must be fruitfully employed.*

*Vidyadhar Nagar incorporates there ideals
along with the needs of contemporary living, working and cultivating spirit.*

*To honour Jaisingh, the main reservoir in
the form of Jal Yantra was created with the
networks of channel for both water-harvest-
ing and distribution.* (B. V. Doshi)

MONUMENTS TIMINGS

Itinerary I: AMER

1. Amer Fort (Amber Palace)
www.amberfort.org
Open: All days (8:00 am - 6 pm)
Night timing (Light Shows)
Holiday: Dhulandi
Entry: Fees
Contact person: Mr. Pankaj Dharendra
+91 0141-2530293
Supam.amber@gmail.com

4. Srijagat Shiromaniji Temple
Open: All days (6:00 am-1:00 pm, 4:00 pm-8:00 pm)
Entry: Free

7. Panna Meena ka Kund
Open: All days (7:00 am-6:00 pm)
Entry: Free

9. Anokhi Museum
www.anokhi.com/museum/home.html
Open: Tuesday to Saturday (10:30 pm-5:00 pm)
Sundays 11:00 am-4:30 pm
Holiday: Monday, National and local holidays
Entry: Fees
Contact: +91 0141-2530226

12. Bharmalki Chhatri (Kachhawa Cenotaphs)
Open: All days (10:00am-5:30pm)
Entry: Fees

13. Hathi Gaon (Elephant Village)
Open: All days (11:30am-6:30pm)
Entry: Fees

Itinerary II: THE WALLED CITY

2. Raj Mandir Cinema
www.therajmandir.com
Open: All days (9:30am-9:30 pm, 4 shows)
Entry: Fees
+91 0141-2374694

5. Museum of Legacies (Rajasthan School of Art)
Opens: Tuesday- Sunday (12:00 noon-8:00pm) Entry: Free
+91 0141-2327020

7. Sargasuli (Isarlat)
www.museumsrajasthan.gov.in/monuments
Open: All days (9:30am-4:00 pm)
Entry: Fees

11. Shri Brijraj Birhariji Mandir
Open: All days (6:00 am - 8:00pm)
Entry: Free

13. Hawa Mahal
www.hawa-mahal.com /
www.museumsrajasthan.gov.in/monuments
Open: All Days (9:00 am - 5:30 pm)
Holiday: Dhulandi. Entry: Fees
Contact person: Ms. Sarojini Chanchlani
+91 0141-2618033
Curmus.hawamahal@gmail.com

17. Jantar Mantar
www.jantarmantar.org / http://museumsrajasthan.gov.in/monuments
Open: All Days (9:00 am - 4:30 pm)
Holiday: Dhulandi
Entry: Fees
Contact person: Mrs. Sashi Prabha Swami
+91 0141-2610494
Supam.jantarmantar@gmail.com

18. City Palace
www.thecitypalacejaipur.com
Open: All days (9:00 am-5:00pm)
Entry: Fees
+ 91-141-4088888

19. Shri Govind Dev Ji Temple
Open: All days (5:00 am-9:00pm)
Entry: Free
www.govinddevji.net

20. Jai Niwas Garden
Open: All days (9:30 am-4:45pm)
Entry: Free

21. Kale Hanuman Ji ka Mandir
Monday- Sunday 5:00 am-1:00 pm, 5:30 pm-10:00 pm
Saturday and Tuesday – 5:00 am-2:00 pm, 5:30 am-11:00 pm
Entry: Free

24. Shri Ramchandraji Temple
Open: All Days (6:00 am-10:30 am and 6:00 pm-8:15 pm) Entry: Free

Itinerary IV:
JAIPUR'S REGIONAL LANDSCAPES

2. Sisodiya Rani Ka Bagh
www.museumsrajasthan.gov.in/
monuments
Open: All Days (8:00 am-8:00 pm)
Entry: Fees
3. Vidhyadhar Ka Bagh
www.museumsrajasthan.gov.in/
monuments
Open: All Days (8:00 am - 5:00 pm and
6:00 pm - 8:00 pm)
Entry: Free
+91 0141-2315714
4. Galta Ji
Open: All Days (5:00 am - 9:00 pm)
Entry: Free
5. Maharaniyon Ki Chhatriyan
Open: All Days (9:30 am - 4:30 pm)
Entry: Free
7. Kanak Vridavan
Open: All Days (8:00 am - 7:00 pm)
Entry: Free
8. Jaigarh Fort
Open: All Days (9:00 am - 4:30 pm)
Entry: Fees
+91 0141-2671848
10. Nahargarh Fort
www.museumsrajasthan.gov.in/
monuments
Open: All Days (10:00 am - 5:00 pm)
Entry: Fees
+91 0141-5134038
11. Gaitor Ki Chhatriyan
Open: All Days (10:00 am - 5:30 pm)
Entry: Fees

Itinerary V:
PUBLIC AND CIVIC ARCHITECTURE

1. Ramniwas Bagh Garden
Open: All Days (9:00 am - 5:00 pm)
Entry: Fees
2. Albert Hall Museum
www.alberthalljaipur.gov.in
Open: All Days (9:00 am - 5:00 pm and
7:00 p.m-10:00 pm)
Holidays: Dhulandi
Last Tuesday of every month (October-
march)
Last Tuesday of every month (April-
September)
Entry: Fees
5. Central Park
Open: All Days (6:00 am - 9:00 pm)
Entry: Free
6. Birla Auditorium
www.birlaauditoriumjaipur.com
Open: All Days (6:00 am - 9:00 pm)
Entry: Free

Itinerary VII:
20th CENTURY JAIPUR - JLN MARG

1. Birla Mandir
Open: All Days (6:00 am - 12:00 pm /
3:00 pm - 9:00 pm)
Entry: Fees
+91 0141-2620969
5. Jawahar Kala Kendra
www.jkk.artandculture.rajasthan.gov.in
Open- All days (10:00 am - 6:00 pm)
Entry: Free
6. Jaldhara
Open: All Days (2:00 pm - 9:00 pm)
Entry: Fees

GLOSSARY

ARCHITECTURAL TERMS AND TYPES

Art Deco. A design style influencing the fields of art, architecture and product design prevalent between the two great wars. Combined modernist functionality with decorative traditions using rich and often colorful finishing materials. Originated in France but spread across the world before modernism became the dominant style in the postwar period.

Ashlar. Masonry work using exposed (random or rectangle) stone blocks on the external face of a brick or stone wall usually plastered from inside.

Baori (sometimes spelled as Bawdi). A manmade stepped reservoir dug deep into the ground for storing rainwater. Excellent example of 'inverted architecture,' where the structure is constructed below the ground level comprising seating areas and resting places that remain (comparatively) cool because of proximity to water and shelter from the blazing sun. Must see (Panna-Meena ka Kund in Itinerary I, for example).

Bazaar. Literally a market or commercial district. But the bazaar is much more than just a physical space. It constitutes the heart of any Indian community whether home or abroad (as in New York's Jackson Heights, Chicago's Devon street or London's Southall). People go to the bazaar to see and be seen, to pick up local gossip or to check out latest fashion and trends, buy, negotiate, and sell. Founders paid special attention to the location and layout of Jaipur's many bazaars that have long served as important economic engines supplying regional, national and global trade networks with diverse products ranging from gems, jewelry, spices, sculptures, crafts and garments. Must see.

Bungalow. Housing typology conceptualized by colonial British in India and then disseminated across the empire. Originally from 'Bangla,' a house with deep verandahs prevalent in the Indian province of Bengal.

Cenotaph. Memorial to commemorate an important and dear person after their death. Employing the *chhatri*, literally an umbrella or domed pavilion, as the basic building block, cenotaphs are typically built on the site of cremation. Characteristic feature of Rajput architecture.

Chaupad. Refers to an indigenous board game of Indian subcontinent but has a special meaning in Jaipur's spatial layout, where it stands for each of the two major extended public squares formed at the intersection of two principal streets respectively, at the heart of Jaipur city. The Badi and Chotti Chaupad (*Badi* means big and *Chotti* means small) are unique to Jaipur (with no parallels in other Indian cities) both exemplifying the city's spatial openness and the designer's cleverness in creating a large and flexible public space used for a range of purposes such as congregation, makeshift bazaar and festivities

Chauraha. Literally the intersection of four streets. Chaurahas serve as important urban nodes attracting diverse activities including bazaars and stops for city buses and rickshaws.

Chemist / Druggist. Means a Pharmacy.

Chhatri. The word *Chhatri* means a canopy or umbrella. 1. It is a consistent architectural element in North-western India and used liberally both in buildings and surrounding open areas, as an open-on-sides pavilion capped by an elevated circular dome supported on pillars. 2. Also signifies a memorial, usually very ornate, built over the site where the funeral (cremation) of an important member of the royal household or a local elite was performed.

Chowk. Open-to-sky courtyard enclosed within a building. Courtyards are a characteristic element of traditional buildings in many parts of North Africa, Middle East and India. Customarily used in Rajasthan's royal palaces and historic buildings due to climatic considerations (facilitating passive ventilation and indirect sunlight, for instance) and cultural functions (such as private use of open space shielded from public gaze). Less frequently but still employed nowadays, largely for aesthetic purposes.

Cinema. Short for a movie or movie-theater.

City Palace. Colloquial term referring to the main royal palace in a city of this region. Usually sited at the heart of urban core from where the settlement developed outwards.

Colony. A new neighborhood or sub-division, usually situated outside the walled city.

Courtyard. See Chowk above.

Darbar hall. Large and usually well-decorated congregation space that traditionally catered to formal meetings of the royal court.

Divider. Road median built in the center of carriageway to divide two-way traffic. Often planted with shrubs or fenced with railing in Indian cities.

Dukaan. A shop. A row of shops on both sides of a street forms a bazaar.

Flat: Means an apartment in a mid to high-rise building.

Footpath. Another name for sidewalk / roadside walkway.

Gali. Refers to a narrow and inner street facilitating access into a dense residential area.

Ghar. Means a house or dwelling.

Guest House. An inexpensive boarding house that provides basic lodging, often coupled with limited eating options. Typically, the guesthouse food is similar to home-made food; the guests here receive relatively more personalized attention than at a hotel.

Gurudwara. Literally house of the Guru. Place of worship for the Sikhs. Usually painted white and topped with a bulbous dome. Jaipur has several with the largest one located in Raja Park.

Haveli. Residential 'type,' or the prototypical unit, that makes-up the bulk of historic Jaipur. Centered upon one or several courtyard(s), a Haveli is an inward-looking building with limited interface with the public street, usually modulated through a series of increasingly private spaces. Must see. (see itinerary 05 for potential places).

Heritage hotel. A historic Haveli, Castle (*Garh*), Fort (*Qila*) or Royal palace (*Mahal*) repurposed as a hotel. Usually involves substantial renovation and redesigning of spaces.

Indo-Saracenic architecture. An architectural style conceived and widely-employed by the colonial British in the late 19th century India. Combined elements from the 'native' traditions and the Gothic revival and Neo-Classical styles favored in Victorian Britain.

Jharokha. An enclosed cantilevered balcony projecting out on a building's higher floor, usually supported by brackets. Jharokha's structure is often constructed with ornately carved stone panels and Jaalis (perforated stone screens that facilitate light and ventilation while ensuring visual privacy).

Kangoora. Refers to parapet wall with successive inverted U-shapes forming a linear silhouette widely-used in forts.

Main Road. The major street of an area. Main roads usually serve as major arterials carrying fast-moving traffic and public transport.

Mandir. A Hindu or Jain place of worship. They vary in size and shape and, patronized by many local communities; are ubiquitous in Jaipur's landscape.

Masjid. Another name for Mosque, which is an Islamic place of worship. Jaipur has several Mosques, but none as elaborate as nearby cities like Delhi and Agra.

Mahal. Royal palace. A Mahal could be a standalone structure or part of a larger complex comprising other buildings as in Jaipur's city palace.

Nala. Natural water channel that drains monsoonal runoff in an area. Frequently used as an open sewer to drain wastewater in many Indian cities.

Paan wala or Paan shop: The ubiquitous jerry-built roadside kiosk selling cigarettes, a range of flavored mouth fresheners, and *paan* -betel leaf wrapped around aromatic spices, and sometimes tobacco, commonly eaten in Gangetic plains. Also, a local informant offering free and useful advice including directions to visiting tourists.

Pol. Entrance gateway (usually framed with an arch) into a city, urban quarter or major building. Sometimes also called Darwaja as in Gangaori Darwaja.

Post-colonial. Refers to occurring or existing imperial legacies after the end of colonial rule. Colonization entailed not only physical control of a territory and its people but also involved fundamentally altering social systems and cultural preferences such as those concerning architecture.

Post-Independence. India gained independence from the colonial British in 1947. The process entailed the amalgamation of more than 550 princely states like Jaipur, and country's bloody partition into the independent states of Indian and Pakistan. The country set out to create a whole range of institutions befitting a modern welfare state; the process influenced and altered many previous practices including the domain of spatial planning and design.

PWD. Acronym for Public Works Department. Set-up by the colonial British both at the federal and state level and entrusted with the whole gamut of civic infrastructure. Engineering-oriented worldview, typically neither known for efficiency nor design sensitivity.

Qila (also called Garh). Fort. Jaipur has several: Nahargarh, Jaigarh and the Amer fort.

Sadak. A road. As you would notice, the road or street is often more than a transportation corridor in the Indian context. It facilitates and brings together a whole range of social activities such as marriage processions, religious parades and weekly bazaars, and service providers like pushcart vendors and pavement sellers—all jostling among the multimodal vehicular traffic.

Saras dairy. The popular sky blue and white color roadside kiosks sell daily needs like bread, eggs, and milk. Sarovar or Jheel. (Usually man-made) Lake.

Subji Mandi. Vegetable and fruit market. The Subji Mandi is a hectic place comprising many vendors squatting under a jerry-built roof on raised platforms as well as pushcarts organized in a large open-to-sky area. Many residents visit the place daily illustrating the centrality of vegetarianism and fresh ingredients in local eating habits.

Sulabh Shauchalaya. Public toilets that charge a small convenience fee and are located in prominent places such as bus stations and major road intersections.

Station. Usually refers to train station. Jaipur has several train stations. If you want to use the metro (Jaipur's light train) ask for metro-station.

Step-well. See Baori above.

Talaab. Pond.

Thadi (with a hard D). A jerry-built roadside kiosk selling chai (tea) and local snacks such as 'biscuit,' or cookies, and Samosas. Cheap and popular venues for a quick drink or bite.

Thana. Police station. Each area / neighborhood has one; usually situated along major roads.

Theka. Means a liquor store. The signboard often carries one or more of the following words 'Wine,' 'English,' 'Beer' and 'Shop'. Open until 8 pm in Jaipur city.

Thela. Pushcart often used as mobile kiosk for vending. You'll find them in Bazaars, Chaurahas and Sabji Mandis. Some Thelas are well-known for selling fast-food items, like poha (a savory snack made with flattened rice) and Omelets. The more popular Thelas are usually easy-to-spot due to large number of people eating there.

Vastu Shilpa. Sometimes also called Vastu or Vastu-Vidya. All these terms refer to traditional knowledges about city-building and architecture documented in ancient treatises. Socio-cultural changes including India's colonization introduced new building practices and preferences relegating these historic ideas and propositions into background. Increasing prosperity and ongoing religious revival has rejuvenated wider public interest in Vastu in recent times.

Zebra crossing. Pedestrian crossing. Always a good idea to check for traffic from all possible directions before crossing a street in India.

GENERALLY USEFUL TERMS AND CONCEPTS

Angrez. Literally an English person but often used generically for white foreigners of any nationality.

Angrezi. English language.

Arranged marriage. A marriage arranged by parents/family members for their children, usually within their own community. Customary manner in which many Indians get married. 'Love marriage,' on the other hand, refers to people findings their own partners and spouses.

Bhagwan. God. Used both as a prefix (as in Bhagwan Krishna) and generically as well.

Bhaiyya. Brother. Also, a commonly employed polite term for calling, or addressing helpers, assistances, waiters, janitors, doormen and taxi drivers.

Block-print. Traditional method employing carved wood blocks to print patterns. Jaipur region is famous for block-printed clothes made using organic colors and cotton fabric.

Bollywood. Hindi film industry, which is one of the world's largest, based in Mumbai. Music and fashion trends from latest Hindi movies dominate the cultural landscape of urban India. Good idea to watch a movie at the Raj Mandir cinema, time permitting.

Chappal. Means flip-flops. Excellent footwear for India's climate barring, perhaps, the short winter period.

Chor. Thief

Cow. Cow is an integral part of Jaipur cityscape. You will find the Gau or Gai (cow's names in Hindi), pronounced 'Guy,' everywhere—on the roads, walkways, and even parks and parking lots. Contemporary Indians have an ambiguous relationship with the cow. On one hand, cow is the holiest animal according to the Hindu tradition, next only to one's own mother. Thus, you will see many people feeding the cows lovingly in public places. On the other hand, customary institutions and practices (such as community-sponsored customary shelters for old cows) have been breaking down in recent times. Thus, you may find old destitute cows feeding on trash with no one to look after them.

Devi (or Maata). Goddess. She is an important Hindu deity representing fertility, mother earth and valor. 'Jai Mata ji' is therefore a popular greeting among many Rajasthanis. You will see many temples dedicated to the Devi's personified human form and many incarnations.

Festival. Religious, communal or family event celebrated with public display of joy and merriment. India has many celebrated through-out the year. For instance, see Gangaur below.

Firang or Firangi. Generic for Europeans. The term has a slight negative connotation due to its association with India's colonial past.

Garba. A dance form originating from the neighboring state of Gujarat but increasingly popular across northern and western India. Offers an opportunity to young people for dancing in a communal setting with members of the opposite sex. Typically organized during the nine-day long Navaratri festival.

Gangaur. A colorful festival celebrating Gauri, the wife of Bhagwan Shiva. Especially prominent in Rajasthan inviting wide public-participation.

Gora. Slang (slightly mocking) for a white person, a foreigner.

Hindu. Believers in a syncretic amalgamation of diverse religious traditions and largely non-doctrinal faiths that developed in this region over centuries.

Hinglish. Contemporary Hindi that uses many English words, several of which are particular to India. For example, words such as 'dicky,' for the trunk of a car, and 'Torch,' for flashlight are peculiar to Indian English. Many urban Indians speak only in Hinglish (and rarely in chaste Hindi or English), which is perhaps the most common language in Jaipur today.

Hindustan. Name for India in Urdu language that means the land or abode of Hindus.

Hindustani. Refers in general to all that which belongs to Hindustan and in particular to a syncretic language that, drawing upon the rich vocabulary and writing traditions of many regional languages including Sanskrit and Urdu, became a common language across many parts of India during the late Mughal and British colonial Period. Perhaps peaked in the films and songs produced around the mid-twentieth century.

Jain. An ancient Indian religion. Followers of 24 Tirthankars, or spiritual thinkers and victorious saviors, who offered a path of charity, kindness and non-violence.

Joota. Shoe or Shoes.

Karma. The idea that what goes around comes around. Morally and ethically appropriate actions would get you good results in future while the inverse would hold equally true.

Krishna. A famous incarnation of lord 'Vishnu,' the god who protects and sustains the world, with many temples in North India including Jaipur. Govind Dev Ji is Jaipur's presiding deity and the daily prayers at his temple in the city's heart provide a spectacular glimpse of devotional religiosity in a public space.

Load shedding (or Power cut). Occasional blackouts due to scheduled maintenance or unexpected breakdowns in the electric grid. Overall Rajasthan state does not suffer from electricity deficit and hence power cuts are rare but not uncommon.

Lakshmi. Goddess of wealth and prosperity, wife of lord Vishnu.

Lift. Elevator.

Mandi. Wholesale market. Jaipur has several Mandis for grains, vegetables and livestock.

Miss (or missed) call. A call that is deliberately cut by the caller before the recipient can answer on a cell phone. Widely used as a signal in Jaipur "give me a missed call when you are ready."

Mobile. Cell phone.

Monsoon. Rainy season, mostly during the months of July-August, that follows the warmest months of May and June. Low-lying parts of Jaipur are prone to rapid collection of surface runoff that could reach 5 to 6 feet of standing water. Stay away from such areas and do not attempt to cross / drive through flooded roads.

Mother tongue. Native language. India has many rich linguistic traditions and it is common to meet many people in large cities like Jaipur who might have a different mother tongue: "I live in Jaipur but my mother tongue is Oriya."

Maa. Mother.

Maharaja / Maharani. Literally the big king or big queen. Highest title in the princely hierarchy, usually reserved for the rulers of largest kingdoms.

Mandapam. Also called mandap. Refers to porch like open hall in Indian temples used for public congregation. Typically supported by exquisitely carved columns depicting deities and legends. Can also denote a pavilion with a plinth wherein Hindu wedding rituals take place.

Mantra. Incantation, usually in Sanskrit.

Mahatma. Great soul, respected human being, often in reference to Mahatma Gandhi.

Mughal. Relating to the Mughal Empire that dominated the Indian subcontinent before the advent of British colonial rule in the nineteenth century. The Mughals were ardent pleasure-seekers developing whole schools of crafts, cuisine and architecture named after them.

Maalish. Massage. Indians have long-mastered the craft of body massage (*maalish*), available in specialized saloons, and head massage (*Champi*) often available in "hair-cutting salons."

Namaste. A greeting, literally "I offer my respects to you."

Pooja (ceremony). A ritualistically-conducted communal prayer usually in a temple or religious gathering.

Rajput. Traditional warriors, rulers and statesmen of this region. Avid builders and naturalists as well. Those with independent estates, or *Jagirs*, carry the titles of Thakur and Raja.

Retiring room. Waiting room for travelers at a train or bus station.

Sadhu. Hindu holy men usually clad in saffron. Often visible in public places seeking alms and small donations.

Taj. A head crown. Also, a short name for Taj Mahal, India's most famous mausoleum in the city of Agra.

Thakur. See Rajput above.

Teej (festival). Refers to a joyous festival, specially celebrated by women, during Monsoons.

Sanskrit. An Indo-Aryan language that originated in the 2nd millennium BCE. Primary scared language of Hinduism that, (like Latin) is rarely spoken, but is the original fount of Hindi and many other regional languages of contemporary India.

Tulsi. An indigenous strain of the herb Basil considered holy by many Hindus. Frequently used as domestic medication for minor ailments like cough and cold.

Vastu. Refers to a set of normative ideas and concepts derived from medieval-period Sanskrit literature dealing with design of buildings and settlements. Efforts to interpret the meaning and purpose of these ancient treatises for contemporary lifestyles have increased with the ongoing revival of Hinduism, the continuing belief that the scriptures offer ultimate solutions and increasing prosperity among Indian middle classes in recent times.

Toilet. Common term used for a restroom or washroom.

Zenana. Sometimes also spelt as Zanana. Relates to females as in 'female restroom' or 'Women's toilet'. Traditionally also used for women's quarters in a fort or palace.

MODES OF TRANSPORTATION

Auto or E-Rickshaw (or Auto in short). Local name for Tuk-Tuk. Readily available at many locations throughout the city and remain a popular mode of transport. Although required to follow a rate-chart, many auto-drivers would name a price after you tell them the destination. Like many monetary transactions in India, negotiating the price is ok both in cultural and practical terms. E-rickshaw is an increasingly common battery-operated version.

Bike. Motorcycle. Light motorcycles are a popular mode of personal transport in Indian cities.

City Bus. The city of Jaipur's bus service offering cheap rides (though often very crowded) that run on fixed routes. These are large buses (compared to Mini buses) and have designated bus stops located through-out the city.

Cycle. Bicycle.

Cycle Rickshaw (or Rickshaw in short). Common term used for human-powered tricycles carrying one or two passengers. Often used for short-distance rides, especially in and around the walled city where other modes of transportation can be difficult to find and navigate.

Ladhha. A cart on wheels pulled by a camel. Popular mode of transporting light goods over short distances.

Metro. Jaipur's new and shiny light-rail commuter system inaugurated in 2015. Presently one line under operation from Mansarovar to the walled city.

Minibus. Privately operated public bus service. Called 'minibus' because of the small-size buses. Frequently painted pink and white, these buses run on many routes covering most of the city. Cheap but usually very crowded.

Taxi. Jaipur offers two types of Taxis: Those booked for day trips or nearby destinations usually through hotel desks or a travel agent on prefixed all-inclusive rates depending upon the make/capacity of the vehicle, and those booked through Web-based Apps such as Uber, Ola and Meru.

Tempo. Colloquial term for Auto rickshaw; also used for small vehicles carrying cargo.

Train. Refers to India's long-distance cheap and reliable rail system called Indian Railways. Jaipur is well connected to many other Indian cities with more than hundred trains leaving from and arriving daily at the 'Jaipur Junction' or 'main railway station.' Several in-bound and out-bound trains also stop at Jaipur's other train stations located at Gandhinagar, Durgapura and Jagatpura.

POPULAR FOODS AND DISHES

Aam. Mango. Come in many varieties as India has some of the best in the World. Unfortunately, they are available only during the summer.

Aaloo-Gobhi. Potatoes (*Aaloo*) and cauliflower (*Gobhi*) cooked together, usually sans gravy. Less spicy compared to most curries. Often eaten with plain Paratha for breakfast or with Dal and Roti for lunch / dinner.

Amrood. Guava. You will see them everywhere in winter months. Locally grown in the region, these are both tasty and nutritious.

Anda. Egg. And chicken eggs are a popular local snack. You will notice roadside carts selling freshly made omelets and boiled eggs on the streets, especially during winter season.

Biscuits. Another name for locally made cookies. Quite popular as a side with hot tea.

Burger. Made up of a vegetable or chicken patty served in a bun. Readily available and quite popular.

Canteen. Cafeteria. Many institutions (like JKK) and colleges (like MNIT) have canteens serving snacks and meals. Reasonable food symbolizing good value for money.

Chai. Pan India name for readymade tea with milk, which is perhaps the most popular drink across the vast country.

Chana or Chhole. Chickpea. Widely available as a spicy curry called Chana masala, often eaten with puffed deep fried bread called Poori for breakfast / anytime meal.

Chawal. Means rice. Not as popular as Roti (Indian bread) in Jaipur cuisine. But most restaurants would have at least one of the following rice dishes: plain rice (straight-up boiled rice), Jeera rice (Cumin flavored fried rice), Pulao or Biryani (yellow rice cooked with vegetables or meat)

Curd. Colloquial for Yogurt. Also called Dahi.

Dal. Refers to a dish made with cooked and sometimes pureed lentils. Tasty and regular part of North Indian cuisine, as well as an important source of protein. Usually comes in two types: yellow dal, which is called 'dal tadka,' and black-brown lentils called dal Makhani.

Dal-Baati. A regional specialty comprising a combination of spicy dal and a sphere shaped hard bread often dipped in ghee (or clarified butter).

Dhokla. A lightly flavored (by Jaipur standards) savory and spongy snack made with fermented batter derived from lentils and rice or chickpeas. Often eaten for breakfast or evening snack, Dhokla is both tasty and nutritious.

Garam. Means hot or warm. Garam chai, for example, means hot tea.

Kachori. A crisp deep-fried puffed pastry made with flour and spicy filling. Two kinds are common: Filled with a lentil mix (*Dal Kachori*) or an onion mix (*Pyaj Kachori*). Usually high on chili but delicious and safe to eat when fresh out of the pan. Easily the most popular anytime snack.

Kela. Banana.

Khana. Food or meal.

Laddoo. A round sweet ball made with chickpea flour, butter and lots of sugar. Comes in several varieties.

Lassi. A sweet and cool drink made with yogurt and sugar; often flavored with rosewater. *Lassi wala* means someone who sells lassi.

Maggi. Refers to a brand of instant noodles owned by Nestle that became widely popular in the 1980s. Available in several flavors even as 'Masala' remains the default option. Treated as a comfort food, eaten both as a snack or a meal by many young and middle-class Indians.

Meat or Mutton. Refers to goat meat with pork or beef usually not available in this part of the world. Mostly curried (in a diverse range of thick or thin gravies) but also used to make tasty kebabs (or kabobs) widely available in many popular restaurants.

Mirchi Bada. One of Rajasthan's favorite snacks made by stuffing a banana pepper with spicy potato filling and then coating with a thick chick-pea batter before deep-frying in boiling oil. Tangy and delicious, especially when freshly made.

Mithai. Sweets. India's take on pastries and baklawas. Rajasthan and especially Jaipur is famous for its hundreds of different kinds of Mitahis made with a combination of milk products, nuts, flour and sugar.

Murgh or Murga. Chicken. A popular item on restaurant menus cooked in variety of ways. Most preparations are delicious, even as 'butter chicken, 'chicken handi,' and 'chili chicken' seem the most popular.

Naan. Freshly made, and one of the rare leavened breads in Indian cuisines, available in most restaurants. Two principal types: Plain Naan (buttered if you ask for 'butter naan') or lightly stuffed with variety of fillings such as spicy onions and crumbled *paneer*- cottage cheese.

Non-Veg. Non-vegetarian food. Goat meat (popularly called mutton), chicken, and eggs are common non-veg options. Fish is available, although important to remember that the state of Rajasthan is largely a desert and the freshness of fish is always dubious. Beef and pork are uncommon as they violate Hindu and Muslim eating codes respectively.

Paani. Water. Usually safe to drink bottled or 'RO' water, which is cleaned through a special filter—ask the server in your hotel/restaurant if they have it.

Pakoda (also called Pakodi). One of North India's favorite snacks that broadly resembles fritters or American 'hush puppies.' Ingredients vary widely depending upon the cook and recipe but typically contain some form of batter, vegetables and spices mixed and deep-fried together.

Paratha. Shallow fried disc-shaped unleavened bread that comes in two major types:

Basic plain version or the one stuffed with a spicy filling such as potatoes (*Aloo ka paratha*), cauliflower (*Gobhi ka paratha*) and onions (*Pyaz ka paratha*). Popular dish for breakfast often accompanying fresh yoghurt and Indian-style pickles.

Poha (or Pohe). Lightly spiced dish (by local standards) made with flattened rice. Often consumed with hot tea on the side, poha is widely available on Thelas, especially popular as a breakfast combo among students and working classes.

Roti. Unleavened disc-shaped bread popular in North India available in two major variations: the crisp Tandoori Roti from the 'tandoor' (see description below) or the soft Chapati from the skillet.

Samosa. Deep-fried triangular pastry filled with savory filling mix of spiced potatoes, onions, peas etc. Sometimes (though rare to find in Jaipur) filled with spicy ground meat. Very popular and tasty midday snack, especially when fresh.

Seb. Apple.

Tandoori. Refers to any food cooked in *tandoor*- a clay oven operating at a very high temperature. Tandoori chicken, Roti and Naan are some of the more popular items cooked in this style.

Thanda. Cold. Colloquially used for soft drinks like Pepsi and Coke products, that are sometimes also called a cold drink.

Veg. Vegetarian food. A substantial section of local population follows dietary strictures, eating vegetarian-only food. Vegetarian food in this part of the World represents a remarkable preference-based cultural tradition where a social group voluntarily rejected all form of meats and eggs developing an unparalleled cuisine based on grains, lentils and vegetables.

BUILDINGS AND PLACES INDEX

FURTHER READINGS

Anand, Mulk Raj. 1977. An Epistle dedicatory to the Master-builder Sawai Jai Singh. *Marg*, Vol. 30

Arora, Ramesh Kumar, Mathur, Shashi and Rakesh Hooja. 1977. *Jaipur: Profile of a Changing City*. Jaipur: Indian Institute of Public Administration.

Borie, Alan, Françoise Catalaa, and Remi Papillault. 2007. *Sommaire Jaipur: Une Ville Nouvelle Du XVIIIe Siècle Au Rajasthan*. Paris: Thalia Edition.

Crewe Quentin. 1985. *Last Maharaja: Biography of Sawai Man Singhji II*. London: Michael Joseph Ltd.

Devi, Gayatri. 1996. *A Princess Remembers: The Memoirs of the Maharani of Jaipur*. Delhi: Rupa and Co.

Dundlod, Harnath Singh. 1970. *Jaipur and Its Environs*. Jaipur: Raj Education Printers.

Hooja, Rima. 2006. *A History of Rajasthan*. Delhi: Rupa and Co.

Horstmann, Monika. 2016. Jaipur's Waterscapes: A Cultural Perspective. *Marg*, Vol. 68.

Jain, Shikha. 2005. *Princely Terrain: Amber, Jaipur and Shekhawati*. Delhi: Shubhi Publications

Kanwar, Dharmendra. 2010. *Gayatri Devi: The Last Queen of Jaipur*. London: White Star publishers

Khangarot, R.S. 1990. *Jaigarh: The Invincible Fort of Amber*. Jaipur: RBSA Publishers

Michell, George and Antonio Martinelli. 1994. *The Royal Palaces of India*. London: Thames and Hudson

Mirza, Ismail. 1954. *My Public Life: Recollections and Reflections*. London: Allen & Unwin.

Nath, Aman and Samar Singh Jodha. 1993. *Jaipur: The last Destination*. Bombay: India Book House

Roy, Ashim Kumar. 1978. *History of the Jaipur City*. New Delhi: Manohar.

Rudolph, Susanne and Lloyd Rudolph. 1984. *Essays on Rajputana: Reflections on History, Culture and Administration*. Delhi: Concept Publications.

Sachdev, Vibhuti and Giles Tillotson. 2002. *Building Jaipur: The Making of an Indian City*. London: Reaktion Books.

Sarkar, Jadunath. 1984. *A History of Jaipur*. Delhi: Manohar Publications.

Shekhawat, Jitendra Singh. 'Heritage Window' column in *Rajasthan Patrika*, Jaipur edition

Singh, Hira. 1998. *Colonial Hegemony and Popular Resistance: Princess, Peasants and Paramount Power*. Toronto: Canadian Scholars Press.

Stern, Robert. 1988. *The Cat and the Lion: Jaipur State in the British Raj*. Leiden: E.J. Brill

Tillotson, Giles. 2007. *Jaipur Namah: Tales from the Pink City*. Delhi: Penguin

ABOUT THE AUTHORS

Growing up in several different parts of India, Pratiksha and Sanjeev studied at the JJ school of Architecture in Mumbai. Providence brought them together at Jaipur after graduating college in 1991. The city had few architects (and fewer in private practice) even as India's emergent economic liberalization was beginning to open up a wide range of opportunities. Taking full advantage of the evolving professional landscape, they worked hard and diligently. Between the two, for instance, they did foundational work establishing Jaipur's leading design practice of the time, and the conception and building of Rajasthan state's first school of architecture; while always finding the time for diverse intellectual pursuits including teaching, traveling, and thinking about the meaning and purpose of design. After the arrival of their lovely daughter Anandita, they have largely lived abroad—beginning with the charming college towns of Leuven, Belgium and Ann Arbor, Michigan before moving to the Great city of Chicago—while returning regularly to Jaipur. This book is special to them not only because it combines discursive knowledges and experiential insights about an architecturally-fabulous place but also because of fond memories and genuine affection for one of the more beautiful cities in the World.

AUTHORS' ACKNOWLEDGEMENTS

This book would simply not exist without the camaraderie of Jaipur's architectural community, many of whom are recognized in Ariadna's note below. But others may have been overlooked inadvertently. To those, our sincere apologies and heartfelt gratitude. Over the years, we have continued to learn about Jaipur from many dear-friends and well-wishers and wish to thank them here. Nihal Mathur, Jaipur native, erudite writer, proud Xavierite and Stephanian, and our beloved Muh-bola Mama, first introduced the walled city and introductory texts in the early 1990s. Benefitting from India's rich oral history traditions, we were lucky to learn about the Jaipur state from affectionate elders like Th. Saheb Ummed Singhji Santha, Th. Saheb Virendra Singhji Khachriyawas, and Lieutenant-general Himmat Singhji Ajayrajpura. Professional collaborations with expert colleagues like Sh. P.K. Jain and design projects with thoughtful patrons like Captain Gaj Singhji Alsisar taught us about traditional design practices and customary construction approaches. Mr. G. S. Nandiwal, from the venerable lineage of Jaipur's accomplished builders and (now-retired) chief town planner of the Rajasthan state, has consistently, and generously, shared his deep knowledge about city's planning history. Young colleagues provided practical help. Suhas [Kothari] helped the project get off the ground, CP [Chandra Pal Singh Bhati] helped with heavy-lifting, and our own Rahul [Singhi] headed the home stretch. Finally, thanks to Vikramaditya (Vikram) Prakash of University of Washington, Seattle for introducing us to Ariadna, whose abiding commitment and indomitable energy saw this project through.

PUBLISHER ACKNOWLEDGEMENTS

As Sanjeev and Pratiksha Ji has mentioned earlier, this book would not have been able to go ahead without the cooperation and friendship of the Jaipur's architectural community. I am especially thankful for their warm welcome and liberal hospitality. First of all, I have to mention the role of two key institutions and their current leaders: The Poornima University and the help of Rahul Singhi, and the MNIT and the guidance of Dr. Tarush Chandra. Rahul guided/lead/managed a team of professors and students who helped with the difficult task of locating and documenting many building plans included in this book. He generously provided logistical support as I needed to visit places and photograph the city. I really admire his personality: a mix of robust kindness and professional efficacy. I also had an exceptional experience with Poornima students who took me to visit many buildings and tourist spots with great enthusiasm and interest: a big thank you to Gaurav Sharma, Shaista Tinwala, Arjun Vishwanath, Shubham Kumar, Sarthak Parnami and Shlok Modi. All of them were guided and encouraged by the ever-smiling Ar. Yash Pratap Singh. And last but not least, thanks to Chandra Pal Singh Bhati who supervised many drawings in the book with consistent patience for all my requests. I definitely could say that MNIT is like my home in the city of Jaipur. Dr Tarush Chandra was always helpful with discussions and arrangements at the MNIT Guest House, where I felt part of the community and was looked after well by the courteous and professional staff. And of course, here I enjoyed the privilege of exploring one of the earliest Kanvinde buildings- the school of architecture, where I was always warmly welcomed by the architectural fraternity.

I would like to mention the exceptional courtesy of Dronah organization extended by Ar. Pooja Agrawal, in letting us use some of their wonderful building drawings, and for sharing with us information about their city Heritage Walks. Aayojan School of Architecture kindly allowed us to use some of their drawings, thanks to the Principal Kiran S. Mahajani and Prof. Archana S. Rathore, In-charge, Documentation Cell. Several other architects including Kavita Jain and Shamini Shankar generously provided us with ideas and material - my sincere gratitude to them. Dharmendra Kanwar was graciously generous in discussing the city's heritage and history, and her book 'Jaipur 10 Easy Walks' helped me to first explore the Walled City. I cannot conclude without mentioning the kind help of Mr Yunus Khimani, Director of the Maharaja Sawai Man Singh II Museum, who took me to explore Jaipur's water heritage structures, along with Gaurav and Shaista to the Jaigarh fort heritage walk on a nice winter morning, carrying with him an iPad containing his wonderful pencil and watercolor drawings.

PICTURES AND DRAWINGS CREDITS

- Albert Hall:
Drawings courtesy Amber Development
& Management Authority (ADMA),
Government of Rajasthan, Jaipur.

- Alsisar Haveli Hotel:
Drawings courtesy School of Planning &
Architecture, Poornima University, Jaipur.

- Amer Fort:
Drawings courtesy Amber Development
& Management Authority (ADMA),
Government of Rajasthan, Jaipur.

- Baradari at City Palace Jaipur:
Drawings ©Studio Lotus
Pictures ©Edmund Sumner, courtesy
Studio Lotus.

- City Palace:
Drawings courtesy Maharaja Sawai Man
Singh II (MSMS-II) Museum Trust, City
Palace, Jaipur.

- Chood Singh Haveli and Hawa Mahal
(elevation and section):

Drawings ©Aayojan School of Architecture
through, Prof. Archana S. Rathore, In
charge, Documentation Cell and her team.

- Gaitore Ki Chattriyan:
Drawings courtesy School of Planning &
Architecture, Poornima University, Jaipur.

- Government Public Library:
Drawings courtesy Gajdhar Associates,
Jaipur.

- Grand Uniara Hotel:
Drawings courtesy Λr. Ankur Tanwar and
Ar. Ruchita Sancheti, Skyline Planners &
Design Developers, Jaipur.

- Hathi Gaon:
Drawings ©RMA Architects
Pictures ©Rajesh Vora, courtesy RMA
Architects

- Hawa Mahal:
Drawings courtesy Aayojan School of
Architecture, Jaipur.

- Jaipur City Plan (pp. 87, 132)
© Rémi Papillault

- 'Jaipur in Princely India before India's
Independence in 1947' map (p. 11)
© Sanjeev Vidyarthi

- Jaleb Chowk:
Drawings courtesy Development &
Research Organization for Nature, Arts &
Heritage (DRONAH), Gurugram

- Lebua Lodge Amber and Lebua Resort:
Drawings and pictures © Amit Mehra,
courtesy Urban Studio

- Malviya National Institute of Technology
(MNIT):
Drawings source Malviya National Institute
of Technology (MNIT), Jaipur.

- Nahargarh Fort:
Gajdhar Associates, Jaipur.

- Pearl institute:
Drawings © Morphogenesis
Pictures ©Edmund Sumner, courtesy
Morphogenesis

- Rajasthan School of Arts:
Drawings courtesy Development &
Research Organization for Nature, Arts &
Heritage (DRONAH), Gurugram.

- Rambagh Palace:
Pictures © Ibai Rigby

- Ram Chandraji Temple:
Drawings courtesy Development &
Research Organization for Nature, Arts &
Heritage (DRONAH), Gurugram.

- Sargasuli:
Drawings courtesy Development &
Research Organization for Nature, Arts &
Heritage (DRONAH), Gurugram

- Sisodia Rani Garden:
Drawings courtesy Development &
Research Organization for Nature, Arts &
Heritage (DRONAH), Gurugram.

- Jaigarh Fort
Digitally recreated by Poornima Team from
Gajdhar Associates, Jaipur, source.

- Tal Katora:
Drawings courtesy Aayojan School of
Architecture, Jaipur.

- Town Hall - Development & Research
Organization for Nature, Arts & Heritage
(DRONAH) , Gurugram

- Tripolia Bazar and Gate - Development
& Research Organization for Nature, Arts
& Heritage (DRONAH) , Gurugram

- Zanana Hospital:
Drawings courtesy Ar. Yash Pratap Singh
Shekhawat and Ar. Chandrapal Singh Bhati.

- Vidyadhar Nagar:
Drawings and text ©Vāstu Shilpā
Consultants (VSF)

- 72 Screens:
Drawings courtesy Ar. Sanjay Puri, Sanjay
Puri Architects, Mumbai.

DOCUMENTATION CREDITS

Head of research team: Ar. Yash Pratap Singh,
Head of Department, School of Planning and
Architecture, Poornima University.

Drawings (digitally recreations by the
School of Planning and Architecture,
Poornima University) and documentation:
Ar Chandrapal Singh Bhati.

School of Planning and Architecture,
Poornima University, Jaipur, students team
(batch 2014-19): Gaurav Sharma, Shaista
Tinwala, Arjun Viswanath, Shubham
Kumar, Sarthak Parnami, Shlok Modi
(Batch 2013-18).

Data research: Ar. Manish, Assistant
Professor, School of Planning and
Architecture, Poornima University, Jaipur,
with the collaboration of Mr. R S Khangarot,
Principal Agarwal College and Dr. Reema
Hooja, Member of the Government of
India's National Monuments Authority.

TEXTS CREDITS

Facts for the visitor text by Ar. Akanksha
Modi, Associate professor, School of
Planning and Architecture, Poornima
University, Jaipur

Glossary text by Sanjeev Vidyarthi and
Pratiksha Singh.

Lebua Resort text by Urban Studio